AWAKE AND ALIGNED

AWAKE AND ALIGNED

*How to Navigate the Human Experience
as a Spiritual Being*

NOVA WIGHTMAN

Printed in the United States of America

First Printing, 2018

ISBN-13: 978-1-947637-92-4 print edition
ISBN-13: 978-1-947637-93-1 ebook edition

Waterside Press
2055 Oxford Ave
Cardiff, CA 92007
www.waterside.com

*To Diggety-Dave, who wouldn't join
any club that would have him as a member.*

ACKNOWLEDGMENTS

I'd like to acknowledge and thank the following incredible beings…

My husband, Trevor–For your support and unwavering certainty in Who I Am and what I am capable of, despite a lot of this not being your particular cup of tea. Your humor, wit, and superpower of lightheartedness instantly plants my feet on the ground, and does more to help me remember Who I Am and what is important in life than anything else. And you're hot. You don't complete me–I am already complete–but man do you enhance me, and I love sharing my completeness with you.

My Mentors–First and foremost, Neale Donald Walsch, for being brave and willing enough to allow the CwG material to come through you and to the rest of us, and for seeing something in me that told you I should come along for this ride. For all you have taught me before I knew you personally, and all you continue to teach me now that we're friends. Next, to Dustin Vice, for being the catalyst for my own conscious journey of aligning with Who I Really Am, and for demonstrating what that looks like, and what life looks like when this happens.

My Cosmic Team–Including my dad, David Schuler. In the physical you were a mentor of mine for sure, my biggest champion and supporter. In the non-physical you are that times a million, and I am so happy to know and experience it.

My Human Team—too many to name but a few I absolutely must: My beautiful, magical mom, Jeanette, who has never allowed me to believe I am anything less than amazing; my older brother, Ned Lucas, who thinks I'm way smarter and wiser than I probably am; my sister, Natalie, who cheers me on no matter what I'm doing; my soul sisters, Lisa, Jennifer, Nicole, Kellie, and Julie, who lent their ears and hearts to me while I moved about this process; my family and friends who allow me to laugh and make fun of life easily, unplugging just enough so that I can consistently plug back in to do this work. And to Emily, Jaime, and Michelle, who diligently and expertly helped me piece together this whole process and all of the words ahead.

And, finally, a deep bow of gratitude to Arlene Mitchell, my friend and treasured consultant, who helped me get my mind wrapped around what I was doing, offering support, feedback, perspective, and validation along the way; you are a Godsend.

TABLE OF CONTENTS

FOREWORD

I don't think it's going to be possible to find, in one place, more immediately helpful, easily usable, and powerfully practical tools for improving one's life than you will find on the pages ahead.

Mind you, I didn't says tools to "make life work," I said tools for *improving* one's life. You're already making life work or you wouldn't even be here, reading these words. But the trick is—after solving the problems and meeting the challenges of basic survival—to improve the *quality* of your life, increase the amount of *happiness* in your life, and experience the tear-producing *joy* in your life of fulfilling the grandest *dreams* of your life.

You didn't come here (to Earth, I mean) to simply meet the needs of your body and satisfy the desires of your mind. Not that there's anything *wrong* with that, but there's so much *more* than that.

This extraordinary book *takes you to The More.*

Nova Wightman here writes with what could almost be called "a flippant grace." There's nothing stilted here, nothing staid, nothing stuffy, stiff, or starchy. Rather, a free-flowing, easy-going, comfort-producing, chuckle-inducing narrative that will take you on a light-stepping walk through what you will surely recognize as parts of your own life, in a way that merrily invites you to *recreate* that life anew—all without a single note of the ponderous in the bargain.

The breadth and scope of the instantly applicable wisdom here, plus the sheer number of approaches and emotional utensils placed before you, may make this the most important book you've ever read.

Add to that the unabashedly candid and unfailingly exuberant tone of the narrative, and you've got what could also wind up being one of the most *enjoyable* books you've ever read.

Okay, Full Disclosure time: I have known Nova Wightman for years. I have been blessed to have her serve our participants as a team member in the Conversations with God Spiritual Mentoring Program. So I can make no pretense of being objective about this remarkable Life Coach and her uncommon ability to be helpful. I'll just tell you, flat out, from my subjective point of view: She's amazing.

But don't take my word for it. Read the book. It's easily a year's worth of coaching that can change your life.

Neale Donald Walsch

"The challenge facing humanity is to close the gap between what the mind imagines itself to know and what the soul actually knows."

~ Neale Donald Walsch

CHAPTER 1
WHO ARE YOU, REALLY?

Have you ever asked yourself, "Who Am I?" Do you feel solid in your answer? This is possibly the biggest question facing humans and, if you are on a spiritual journey, one you are, likely, not taking lightly. I trust that is why you have picked up this book today.

Who You Really Are is an extension of the Source, of God, of the All That Is. In other words, you are more than just human; you are more than what you see. You are not just your body, you are not just your mind, but you are not just your soul, either. You are a combination of all three.

"Who You Really Are" is *God expressed in individuated form*. Yet, most of us have been raised to think that such a thought is blasphemous or impossible, and therefore we have lived the majority of our lives in direct conflict with our true nature and essence. And that's really painful.

For those of you who feel you do know Who You Really Are, or are at least on the path of embracing my above description, do you often find yourself struggling to actually *be* and *express* that highest version of yourself within the

1

apparent confines of everyday human life? I'm betting you do, or you have, otherwise you wouldn't be reading this book. Look, it's tough, I get it. I get that it's difficult to take a resonant, joyful spiritual concept and truth and turn it into practical, life experience. I get that you have over 60,000 thoughts in a day, most of which are subconscious, that you struggle to sift through, feeling confused about which ones are "real" and which ones are not. I understand what it's like to feel like you have so many pieces of the spirituality puzzle, yet don't quite have a clear picture of how to put them together into a cohesive life plan.

If you found your way to a book like this, I'm guessing that you've been swimming in the deep waters of spiritual concept long enough to feel frustrated with your own ineffectiveness; you know intrinsically, passionately, and with certainty that there is more to life than what the general public sees and experiences, and you are ready to put what you know into practical use. I'm also guessing that, in your conscious spiritual journey, you find yourself having very human moments, and you struggle to accept and love those human aspects of yourself; you struggle to see these parts that most would never describe as spiritual, or even deserving of love and acceptance, as a valid part of Who You Really Are.

This book will empower and embolden you who know that we are all limitless, powerful beings who possess the tools and abilities to create the lives we truly desire, yet are not quite sure how to harness that knowledge into momentum. This book is for you who are bursting at the seams to be Who You Really Are, to declare, express, and experience your utter magnificence, but can't yet define what that looks like. This book is for you who know intuitively that life doesn't have to be so damn hard, who believe in magic, and want to see it in action on a daily basis.

It is my hope and intention that this book wakes up those who are half asleep, that it makes a gigantic contribution to the consciousness and vibration of the world, raising us all up by way of raising the vibration of the individual. Abraham-Hicks (a group consciousness from the non-physical dimension translated by speaker and author, Esther Hicks) says that one who is in alignment with Who They Really Are is more powerful than a million people who are not, and their energy indeed empowers those others. They have also said that the greatest gift you can give another is your own happiness.

I have found both statements to be extremely true. I know how overwhelming it can feel to look at the state of the world, or one of the seemingly endless heart-breaking aspects of human life, and feel totally and utterly helpless. What can I do? What kind of impact can one single person make? I tell you, you can make the biggest impact of all. It just takes one domino to knock over the rest, one tiny pebble skipped across the water to create the ripples. One person can cause an avalanche of goodness in the world and not even be aware of it. Happiness, love, and joy are contagious, and that is exactly what this world needs.

...And who the hell am I?

I have one foot firmly planted in the physical world and the other foot dancing in the spiritual realm. I am a mom, a wife, a Tae Kwon Do Master, an energy-worker, a smart-ass, and both a spiritual student and teacher. I felt compelled to bring forth this book, a practical guide to living your life as your highest, most authentic self, because of my ability to navigate life's mundane and mystical aspects, as well as my ability to teach those notions through my coaching practice. When you follow the guidance that follows here, applying the practical steps to bring your actions into line with your own stated beliefs about yourself, a magical thing occurs: that separation between Who You Really Are and who you think you should be disappears, and life flows better. By being willing to do the challenging work of self-exploration and examination, you, too, can navigate and merge your physical and spiritual identities with ease.

Merging my own humanity and spirituality looks a little something like this: I am a spiritual Life Coach, running my own business as well as working on the *Conversations with God* coaching team. I also love watching *The Walking Dead*.

I spend most of my days helping others find connection and higher meaning in their lives, and, almost simultaneously, chasing a 2-year-old to wipe her runny nose. I am often balancing contemplating life's deepest meanings with unraveling the tangles of my 6-year-old's hair, amidst her feigned objections of pain. I am equally overwhelmed with awe and wonder at the wisdom of the world's many great teachers as I am when sitting with the love of my life, watching our two amazing little girls point and giggle at each other in delight because they are both wearing their hot pink, fuzzy bath robes.

Like you, I am a spiritual being having a very human experience and I am constantly working towards closing that gap between my spirituality and humanity, striving to be Who I Really Am in the most basic of ways. I mean, it's difficult enough to conceptually grasp the magnificence of Who We Really Are; it's a whole other ball game to make it work in this very human arena in which we live, navigating the countless distractions and things that appear at first glance to be working against us.

I am challenged to remember and lean into the concept of "We Are All One" when the person I am holding the door open for gives me a dirty look instead of a "thank you." I jump for joy in those moments that I finally "get" something or receive a timely reminder of what I already know deep inside, and I have often fallen flat on my face, sometimes even chipping a tooth, when attempting to apply it to "the real world." How many moments like this, when your intentions haven't quite materialized the way you intended, have you experienced? I'm guessing you can relate.

Why living your spiritual truth, instead of just talking about it, really matters

I attended a *Conversations with God* retreat in the fall of 2006, something I had always wanted to do since first discovering the books. The name of the retreat was "Living Your Purpose" and incidentally, that is where I found my purpose: Life Coaching. Actually, please allow me to amend that statement. I found the next application and modality for my purpose, as I am now clear that my purpose is to be Who I Really Am and enjoy the process of defining, expressing, and experiencing that. Life coaching was a relatively new profession which I didn't know existed, and which could allow the aspects of Who I Really Am, called healer, teacher, guide, bringer of light, etc., to be expressed. I was ecstatic!

Those first several years I played around with my focus for how I was going to help others, trying on such niches as work/life balance and financial abundance coaching. But they were all short-lived and ultimately led me to one very powerful and compelling message that touches the heart of every soul on this planet: **Being Who You Really Are.**

Put another way, I was helping others identify who they were as spiritual beings and as human beings. I was helping them merge the two, functionally, to bring more peace, fulfillment, satisfaction, harmony, and joy to their lives. I noticed early on that no matter what my clients came to me for, be it work-life balance, life-purpose, or improving their relationships with money, they were all practically begging for the same thing. They wanted to live authentically, intentionally, consciously, and freely. Isn't that what we all want?

Admittedly, I was not the best at this right off the bat. I had a lot to learn, but I made enough of an impact to help my clients see some awesome changes in the quality of their lives. Over time, I began to identify and piece together the parts of my work and the resources I used that were the most effective in accomplishing and experiencing my clients' goals.

I was a talented yet unsuccessful coach and entrepreneur, and the most common descriptive word you could use to describe my career at the time was "almost." Ultimately, in 2011, I hired a coach and mentor, who gave me the most powerful ingredient I had been missing. I had so many pieces of the puzzle, and I even had some of them put together in a shape that vaguely began hinting at the big picture. But I was missing one huge necessary and vital piece: **alignment**. That is, coming from a place of alignment with Who I Really Am in everything I do.

I quickly learned that alignment was the key to turning the word "almost" to "always." My coach taught me about the power of aligning with Who We Really Are. He also gave me the practical tools for which I had always yearned. I have to tell you, this was without a doubt the most significant turning point in my career and in my whole life. I began to *get it.* And more importantly, I began to *apply it to my own life consistently.*

This is where I made my biggest leap yet. Over the course of less than six months of focused energy, intentions, and habits I aligned with my Highest Self more than ever before. As a result, I consciously transformed and co-created my career, relationships, finances, and personal life. I witnessed and danced with the magic of the Universe, catching indescribable glimpses of what is possible in this beautiful life. I felt deep contentment, satisfaction, fulfillment, and trust. The feeling of certainty became a familiar friend. More on all this will be discussed later.

Perhaps most unexpectedly, yet delightfully satisfying–I began to really, really enjoy my humanity. My humanness, that is, the parts that most would say are the parts we should "fix" or "rise above." The best part of this work for me, the most exciting thing I hope you learn to embrace through your work in this book is that, in aligning with Who You Really Are, you begin to see that there is nothing to fix at all. There is just more to enjoy and love, and you naturally begin to stop condemning these parts of yourself, embracing them more fully, instead.

A method to my madness

I don't want to be vague about any of this. There's nothing more frustrating than someone promising you the keys to everything you've ever wanted and then not being clear on how to use them. So, I will share some of my experiences, my story, as well as the stories and experiences of others who have consciously walked the path of alignment, to help put some specific and downright magical concepts into context for you, so that you may render them functional in your own life.

I will include a "practical application" tool in each chapter, and I highly recommend you actually do them. To give you an idea of how important the action part is, everything you read in these pages I have known consciously to some extent for the better part of my 35 years on this planet, but it was only in the last 5 years that I actually began to put them into practice and this is when I really experienced any real success. And remember, I had to hire a very expensive coach to help me do it (totally worth it, of course).

But this is a book, and you are likely reading it on your own. So find a way to kick your butt into gear and put these tools to use. Find a way to hold yourself accountable–to your *self*. After all, there is a reason you are here in this moment, with this book in your hands. Consider that your soul, your Higher Self, or whatever language you hold around this concept, has placed you in this exact moment, in your exact circumstances, with your exact challenges and blessings for a purpose. This is precisely what you needed to point you, and indeed, place you, where you are going. A certain life-long mentor of mine offers this unique perspective in most, if not all, of his books and it gets me every time. Because he's absolutely right. Life is always working for us, guiding us along through small and large prompts, urges, whispers, and sometimes frying pans to the head.

What would change for you if you deeply believed and knew this? What if you knew beyond a shadow of a doubt that this is your time, this moment is *the moment* your soul has been guiding you to all along? What will it be like, feel like, to finally begin merging with the magnificent being you've always suspected you are?

What that all looks like for you is, well, up to you, but know that this moment is a *huge* stepping stone. By following the prompts in the pages ahead, understand that Life, as you know it, is about to drastically change. Get ready for your leap.

What You Need To Know Moving Forward

Because they are the premise of this book and the terms will be used repeatedly, let's clarify what I mean by "spirituality" and "humanity." "Spirituality" is self-awareness, awareness of your connection to the world around you, and that something bigger than you exists. It is about consciously remembering, discovering, and creating Who You Are and what you believe versus simply adopting an existing set of beliefs without stopping to see if they actually resonate with you. Being spiritual doesn't necessarily mean that you don't go to church or identify with a certain religion. It means you are active in your awareness of what you are hearing and being exposed to, giving more weight to what you feel than what you are told.

"Humanity" refers to the very human aspects of life, and ourselves, from our perceived "flaws" to the everyday dealings and contexts we come across. It is what some people might refer to as "reality."

I will also be using the words and phrases "being Who You Really Are," "merging your spirituality with your humanity," "alignment," and "well-being" frequently. Please be aware that I use them interchangeably as well. They convey the same thing, as they all carry the same essence and energy.

While these concepts are undoubtedly familiar to you, I hope to convey them in a way that will assist you in applying them, practically and functionally, in your own life. It is not necessarily my intention to guide you to the top of the mountain to sit with Buddha, meditating endlessly for the rest of your existence in a supremely serene and connected state of being, but rather to guide you on those rougher trails way down below, making them more enjoyable and smooth. I want to help you feel okay with being down there in the first place and invite you to take your time. I strongly believe in following the path of "meeting yourself where you're at" versus trying to make an unrealistic leap to the top and beating yourself up for missing the mark. We came into our human form for a reason, which I believe is to play and express and experience ourselves in the countless and endless ways we've been given to do so. There's no need to rush that.

There are certain assumptions and beliefs assumed going forward that would be helpful for you to know at the outset. While they are considered common in the spiritual development community, as well as my own approaches, they are offered as merely "my take" on it. It is important to note that I am not offering any of these concepts as "the way," but merely "another way." This type of spiritual knowledge is heavily reliant on the person taking what fits and disregarding what doesn't; so I encourage and invite you to take what resonates and works for you and discard the rest. But, you did pick this book up for a reason, so while I expect many readers already know and accept the premises below, if you don't, I encourage you at least try on the ideals presented so that you know more about who you are and how you operate.

For foundational purposes, here are a few of the spiritual assumptions we are operating within in this book:

- Everything is energy. We are first and foremost vibrational beings, extensions of Source/God energy.
- Thoughts are creative and are behind every single thing we see in our world.
- What you pay attention to and give energy to is what you will invite more of into your experience.
- We are the creators of our own reality. More specifically, we are the co-creators of the events or things that show up in our lives and world, and are the sole creators of our experience of it all.

- We came into our physical bodies so that we can express and experience Who We Really Are through the contexts and contrast of physical life.

Finally, this book is divided into five parts:
- Part 1: Alignment
- Part 2: Embracing Your Humanity
- Part 3: Embracing Your Spirituality
- Part 4: Stories of Alignment
- Part 5: How to Be Who You Really Are

Part 1 is designed to give you a clear understanding of what alignment means for you and your life, and building a foundation for it. Part 2 takes a deeper look in what it means to be human, why that's not a bad thing, and what can happen when you embrace this integral part of yourself. Part 3 focuses on the aspects of yourself that are more "spiritual," and how to embrace and integrate them in your everyday life. Part 4 gives you real-life stories and examples of what life can look like when you connect and align with the highest version of yourself. And finally, Part 5 takes you into the nuts and bolts of how to bring it all together to enjoy your life as Who You Really Are.

Many of the focuses of each chapter could easily go into one or more of the other parts, as a lot of these concepts overlap, and there is a lot of repetition with some of the more vital concepts. This is a good thing, and isn't meant to annoy you. It is meant to further and more deeply integrate these truths into both your conscious and unconscious minds, to make the whole process more effortless.

I highly suggest that you dedicate a notebook, journal, or word document to your experience of reading this book, as there are many exercises and tools offered that will be easy for you to say, "That sounds like it will really help me! I'll do it later…" and then never come back to it. The seed will be planted and your consciousness will inevitably change simply by reading these words and beginning the process of simply thinking in a new way. However, if you are really ready to let that soul of yours take the driver's seat, do the work as we move along.

Now, let's dive in!

PART 1:
ALIGNMENT

Alignment is your access point to being Who You Really Are. Get into a state of alignment, and you won't have to think or try very hard to be your Highest Self. In this section, I am going to help you understand this concept more deeply, and help you lay the foundation for living a life of alignment with Who You Really Are. There are some very powerful exercises offered to assist you in this, but I've also included my story to help illustrate some pretty heady concepts. I'm a pictures and examples gal, so I really appreciate hearing how things apply in real-life terms. I'm assuming many of you will, too.

CHAPTER 2
ALIGNMENT OR BUST

"If you want to awaken all of humanity, then awaken all of yourself. If you want to eliminate the suffering in the world, then eliminate all that is dark and negative in yourself. Truly the greatest gift you have to give is that of your own self-transformation."

~ *Lao Tzu*

By now you've already heard me use the word "alignment" quite a few times. When I use that word in a book like this, you likely have at least a vague idea of what I mean by it. But because I believe this to be the magical ingredient to being Who You Really Are, it's important to have as clear of an understanding as possible.

Alignment is the key to everything. Understanding it and how to consistently live in a state of alignment is hands down the single most important thing you can do for yourself, and even those you love. It is where all miracles, magic, manifestation, and good things begin and end. In other words, how much or how often you are in alignment directly relates to your level of happiness and satisfaction in your life. It's also referred to as "being in the flow," "being centered and connected," "being Who You Really Are," and for all you Abraham-Hicks fans out there, "being in the vortex." It is feeling clear, inspired, certain, and confident that *anything* is not only possible, but that you are capable and deserving of it all. It is the keen awareness that you are a part of, indeed one with, something much bigger than yourself. Some call it "God-consciousness," and of course, there are different degrees of it.

Perhaps the simplest way I can describe a state of alignment is when you find yourself feeling really "good." Good is a broad, general term, of course, and there are different levels of feeling good so I'll give you my own definition: It is when you feel clear, connected, and happy. You can also look at it as a gauge: how good you are feeling is indicative of how much you are currently in alignment. When you find yourself not feeling so great at all, whether physically, mentally, emotionally, or spiritually, consider yourself as being out of alignment or out of the flow. This isn't a bad thing, and it's not even necessarily a result of something you've done "wrong," although there are definitely practices that do and don't support your alignment.

Going in and out of alignment is a very natural and normal thing for every human on this planet. It is a part of life, and life itself has a natural ebb and flow to it. *Perhaps to your surprise, the goal is not to stay in alignment 100% of the time. In fact, I believe that to be impossible and not actually in our best interest. The goal is to live a life of alignment most of the time, and know what to do to get back into alignment once you are out of it.*

I can't tell you how much I wish I had known and understood this in the earlier parts of my search. I'm not sure where I got the idea that it had to be 100% of the time or else, but that was certainly the perspective I was living in, and it caused a lot of self-judgment and disappointment. Ironically, even in the early days of my work, I never once expected any of my clients to be "on" 100% of the time. Funny how we tend to set ridiculous standards when it comes to ourselves. Fortunately, now I not only know that 100% alignment, consciousness, awareness, and connection is not the goal; I understand that there is great value in those "out of alignment" moments. Dare I say? I've even learned to enjoy them every once in a while! I believe the goal is to learn to embrace those moments we are out of the flow, when we are experiencing contrast or difficult situations, thoughts, and emotions. It is to learn to recognize that they, too, are an important part of the human experience and opportunity. They, too, are a gift.

Alignment and Contrast

Let's talk about that now, shall we? If you are unfamiliar with the word "contrast" in this context, I am using it to describe the not-so-enjoyable stuff of life like pain, suffering, heartache, bad experiences, challenges, and difficulties. We live in a world where everything is relative, so we need that contrast in order to have certain experiences, or experience certain aspects of ourselves. *Conversations with God: Book 1*, by Neale Donald Walsch, gives the best explanation of this that I have come across and I highly recommend you pick up a copy or reread it. Put simply, one can't know oneself as tall in the absence of short, as good in the absence of evil, or as successful without the knowledge or experience of failure.

Furthermore, it is in those moments of contrast that we become clearer than ever about what it is we want in life and who it is we want to be. Abraham-Hicks describes this as "launching a rocket of desire" in the very instant we are experiencing something we don't like or want. With this understanding in mind we can give ourselves permission to embrace each experience and event in life because it will always present us with the gift of clarity and the opportunity to do things differently.

Allow me to give you an example of this to which I'm sure many will relate. One recent December, I found myself overwhelmingly busy, with more on my plate than the usual holiday hustle and bustle. I had a packed client load, several big projects that needed my attention, time, and energy, plus family commitments. I was hosting three parties at my house that month and we had just moved in, for Pete's sake! I want to say that I don't know what the heck I was thinking during that time, but in retrospect I can see it perfectly: I was making decisions from a place of obligation and skewed perspective vs. from a place of calm, centered, clear alignment. It was the kind of busy that wasn't fun anymore, and I found myself counting down the days to Christmas, not for the joy of the holiday, but for the craziness to stop. In fact, I didn't really get to tune into the magic of the season at all, which is something I treasure and value very much.

The final straw was in the middle of the month when I landed myself in the ER due to a case of severe stomach flu and a cyst bursting on my ovary. It was some of the worst pain of my life. Fortunately, I recovered quickly and, although I was asking myself the age-old question of "why did this happen?", I did know one thing for sure: I was never going to repeat this experience again.

From that very strong experience of contrast and general suckiness, I became crystal clear that in the future I wanted to take the entire month of December off. I made the decision right then and there that from then on I would not take on any new projects late in the year, and would keep hosting and social events to a minimum. I even wrote notes about these desires in my journal and my calendar for the following year, and changed my next year's experience completely. I had a wonderfully slow, intentional, and present December. I honored my desire to take time off of work and actually didn't host one party. And no ER visits! It was wonderful, and it was because of the very unpleasant experience the year before that I was able to consciously create that.

So, contrary to popular limiting belief, the so-called "bad stuff" of life is actually a very necessary part of our human and spiritual experience, providing us with tools to use for some pretty amazing growth, if we are aware and intentional enough. Sometimes we can't see the other gifts and opportunities right away, and that's okay. It is during those times that I choose to remind myself that I don't need to know yet and that I trust in the divine, perfect order of things. I also try to remind myself that challenge creates an opportunity for expansion. We'll go into a bit more detail on the gifts and opportunities of contrast and negativity and how to use them later.

The Payoff

Engaging in the work of being Who You Really Are can be some of the most challenging work you will ever do, even if from the outside it doesn't look like you are doing much at all. But because it takes your almost constant focus, attention, and awareness, not to mention willingness, to shift out of negative thought patterns or actions that are not serving you, it can seem exhausting at first.

So what's the payoff? Tell me, if you are interested in:

● Having things fall into place for you, all the time, with very little effort on your part?

● Being constantly flooded with ideas, inspirations, answers, solutions, opportunities, insights, and divine nudges?

- Naturally looking at life from a positive vantage point and embracing everything that shows up as something that supports your higher purpose, experiencing almost instant peace in the face of things that would have dismantled you in the past?
- Finding yourself better equipped to handle and manage the "down" times, even turning the bad experiences into good ones?
- Feeling physically, mentally, emotionally, and spiritually healthy, strong, and happy most of the time?
- Being known as the guy or gal who always has a smile on his or her face?
- Really, truly, and actually loving and liking yourself, and not being ashamed to own that?
- Enjoying your life and the pleasures of this world more deeply and guilt-free?
- Having happier, healthier, more mutually beneficial, and fulfilling relationships?
- Seeing situations more clearly, and understanding others with more compassion and empathy?
- Becoming clear on your purpose and acting on it?
- Having pleasure, play, and fun be a necessary part of your day and feeling good about that?
- Moving about your life with ease, joy, peace, contentment, passion, compassion, and authenticity more often than not?
- Being sought after in your work instead of you doing all of the seeking?
- Experiencing miracles, magic, manifestation, serendipity, and synchronicity as everyday occurrences?
- Becoming more in tune to your innate gifts, strengths, and abilities *and* discovering what other ones may be lying dormant within you?

- Being in intentional and conscious communication with your spirit guides and angels?
- Experiencing ever-expanding amounts and forms of pleasure, happiness, and love?
- Implicitly trusting in yourself, in God, and in the Universe and moving about your life in the energy of certainty?
- Finally understanding that you don't actually need anything outside of yourself in order to be happy? That it's not really about the car, the job, the house, the money, the relationship, the family, etc., but how you think they're going to make you feel?
- Understanding that you can actually be happy, now, for no reason at all, and as a nice side effect all of those things will come into your experience anyway?

I'm guessing most of that sounds good to you, if not amazing. All of those things and more flow into your experience more easily and noticeably when you learn to live in alignment consciously and consistently. This is because, energetically speaking, you are leaving the door open for the Universe to deliver on all of the above items more frequently.

The Cost

What does it cost you when you are not in alignment? Well, the big answer is nothing. Misalignment is a necessary part of the equation as there is no greater joy than the feeling of being swept back into the flow when you've been out of it for any measure of time. Remember, we live in a yin and yang sort of world where we need a bit of that contrast in order to really experience and know the best life has to offer. But for the purposes of this conversation, it will cost you everything on the list above, at least for a little while, until you are, inevitably, brought back or work your way back in to alignment (I'll show you how to do this in a later chapter). Even those who have never heard of or will never hear of and/or be interested in any of this stuff will experience the ebb and flow of alignment on a day-to-day basis. You can't escape it. It's how life and energy work.

The invitation I am extending to each of you reading this is to use this information to your advantage. I invite you to embrace this concept and all that follows in the pages ahead as a key to finally unlocking how to make your life work the way you want it to, in order to finally achieve your idea of success and happiness. During the first years of my coaching business there was next to nothing intentional about my own alignment, so my experience was more or less like trying to swim upstream. Once I understood the power of alignment and aligning with Who I Really Am, it quickly began to feel more like a nice, leisurely float downstream as I took in all of the sights.

The truth is, once you experience and become aware of this alignment business, it's really hard to go back to the way you were living before. Ask any of my clients or anyone who has come across this particular approach how they feel after a few days of ignoring their daily practices and they'll tell you it's hugely uncomfortable, even painful. Most will say they have a lower tolerance for the former chaos, confusion, and discomfort they used to feel prior to this work, which acts as a natural motivation to keep them on course.

I'm going to share with you some very specific techniques and practices you can do to foster this foundation of alignment that will help make it a way of life, and I know firsthand that when I skip doing these things for any length of time I feel it, and it does not feel good. Once you know what you are doing you sort of become addicted to alignment–addicted to feeling good and the experience of being and expressing your true self. But trust me, it's not a bad addiction to have.

In Case You're Still Not Clear on this Topic

At one point, I hired someone, Dustin Vice, to help me fully integrate what I already knew conceptually about life, alignment, and energy, as well as teach me some of what I didn't yet know and apply all of it to my daily life in a very functional way. He is author of *"Making Waves: How to Build a Successful Coaching Business During the Coaching Tsunami,"* owner of Alliance Coaching Systems, and physical embodiment of most of the things I had wanted to become in life. He ended up being a major catalyst in my transformation and as a result of his coaching, my life quickly and drastically changed for the better. Naturally, I asked him to share his own definition and thoughts on alignment to help you further understand this concept:

> *"Alignment is the state where your conscious mind and your unconscious mind are working together, overall in harmony, to allow your physical self to create the experience for your non-physical self to come through and to learn, grow, and play to expand, as it intended before arriving here, through this life experience. How do you know when you are in this powerful, aligned state? You feel good, really, really good. The better you feel the more in alignment you are. It is that simple.*
>
> *Now many, no wait, all of us need to learn how to create a relationship with the unconscious, consciously, and with the non-physical self to create the flow of feeling good, really good, more of the time. Now you may have noticed that I used the word "more" and not "most". The reason I say*

that is because you cannot escape the pain in this world, it is inevitable and its purpose is to offer to you an experience to grow powerfully. You cannot live in pure bliss for your entire life. Therefore it is good to have a realistic goal in mind to prevent yourself from experiencing unnecessary disappointment. Create the intention to feel good more of the time.

Create the intention to learn and master how to consciously influence the patterns of your unconscious to shift old beliefs, bad habits, and to allow your soul to come through, to learn, and to grow. Create the intention to connect to your true self. Create the intention to open to your heart and allow it to lead you on this journey to merge fully with your soul and to grow in the deepest part of your whole self. I promise you will not be disappointed.

There will be moments when it will be difficult and you may wonder what have I got myself into? It will be worth it and your life will become more fun, more enjoyable, and wealthier in all senses of the word as a result of your intentions. Your roles in life will change over time; it is important not to confuse them as your purpose. Understand your purpose for this life is simple, for your soul to create, expand, and to grow. Enjoy the ride. Feel good. Have fun. Indulge in the moments of life's gifts. Get through the suffering of the pain as quickly as possible. Cherish the ones you love and above all else love yourself and make feeling good your top priority, your number one job, your mission. That is my definition of Alignment."

Practical Application:

Let's take a little evaluation of your life in terms of alignment and feeling good in order to meet you where you are, yes? Without judgment of what is so, rate yourself on a scale of 1-10, 1 being not at all and 10 being all the time, on how often you believe you are in a state of alignment with Who You Really Are. What would it take to get that number to be one number higher? How committed are you to doing that? Write your answers in your journal.

Next, begin a daily gratitude and appreciation practice. Gratitude and appreciation are the quickest and perhaps most effective ways, of which I am aware, to help you feel good and consciously get into a state of alignment. We will cover this concept in greater detail towards the end of this book, in Part 4: How to Be Who You Really Are, but for now just start with writing down five things you are grateful for each day. The only requirement of this exercise is that you choose things that you truly feel grateful for or appreciative of, and that you feel it in the moment you are writing it. So avoid writing down canned answers or things you think you "should" feel grateful for, and choose the things that are easy to access, no matter how seemingly small. It's also helpful to choose a person or situation in your life that is easy to feel good about, and list five things you are grateful for about him/her/it.

This isn't a one-time exercise, by the way. I used the word "daily" for a reason, and if you're serious about this aligning with Who You Really Are business, I highly recommend that you adopt this as a daily practice. It not only feels wonderful, but it is an active ingredient in drawing wonderful things to you.

CHAPTER 3

SYMPTOMS OF ALIGNMENT

"The soul always feels joy, because the soul is joy. The soul always feels love, because the soul is love. The soul always feels connected with the wonder of life, because the soul is the wonder of life, expressed. In order to feel this always, you have to be out of your mind. You have to get 'out of your head' and into your heart."

~ *Neale Donald Walsch*

In my nine years of professional life coaching and my over 20-year quest for being Who I Really Am, I've noticed a few things about those who have achieved a significant degree of living in alignment with Who They Really Are. I say a "significant degree" versus just flat out full achievement, because it is certainly an on-going journey of expansion, growth, and remembrance, with plenty of "forgetting" in the mix. As Abraham-Hicks loves to say, "You can't get it wrong and the work is never done." These individuals I have come across that either already had it or grew into it right before my eyes all shared some very specific things, and I should note that they would identify themselves as highly spiritual people, so the language I am using below is their language (and mine).

To be fair, I believe there are plenty of people on this planet who are pretty darn good at being who they came here to be who would stare at you blankly if you used the language below. No matter how you describe it, authentic living is free of resistance, appears effortless and natural, and it is clear the individual is comfortable in his or her own skin. But to stay congruent with the theme and language of this material we're going to go the metaphysical route.

I really enjoy it when personal and spiritual development books offer a list of specific examples to illustrate what one might notice upon applying the specific principles and techniques offered. Brené Brown does this in many of her books that focus on her main concept of "wholehearted living," giving a detailed list of what living this way looks like. I took great pleasure in listening to her audiobooks and recognizing the aspects that I already have or have begun integrating into my experience. The parts that I haven't yet identified with gave me a clear idea and direction of where to look next, which is beyond awesome for a spiritual development junkie such as myself. So, I'm going to do you the same favor.

From a place of as little judgment as possible, read the list below, paying attention to which ones are present or are emerging in you, and which ones are not there yet. Remember, "you can't get it wrong and the work is never done!" This is fun for our souls! (Although not always for our human selves.) Use it as a guidepost to see which areas are calling for your attention, and be sure to give yourself some big-time acknowledgement for the aspects that are already present and being expressed within you. Do not be afraid to do that. I assure you it is not arrogant. When we claim and celebrate the best parts of ourselves, we have the pleasure of watching them expand and multiply!

The following is nowhere near a comprehensive list of habits, beliefs, and attributes held by those living in consistent alignment with Who They Really Are and, like I said, are mostly based on my experience and observations. It is also important to note that the following are experienced in different degrees and, no matter where the aligned being falls within that, it is a work in progress. Finally, keep in mind that we will be addressing many of these points in fuller detail in the chapters ahead.

Attributes of those living in alignment with Who They Really Are:

- *They engage in a set of daily practices that are soul-nourishing and support their well-being, knowing that this is the foundation of their alignment.* This is their top priority and the place they always return to when they find themselves feeling lost or are in a moment of "forgetfulness."

- *They consistently practice gratitude and appreciation.* Even though the contents of their daily practices may differ, they all actively acknowledge what they are grateful for and appreciative in life, as it is the number one tool to get one into a higher state of being.

- *They do not need anything outside of themselves in order to be happy, feel good, or experience any variation of that, although they do have preferences.* They deeply recognize that it is not the job, the house, the car, the relationship, the money, etc. that they want; rather what they want is how they think those things are going to make them feel. They recognize and believe that we all have the ability and constant opportunity to feel good right now, independent of anything external, and they strive to practice this as often as possible.

- *They strive to embrace every single event and circumstance that shows up in life as being there to serve their highest purpose, even if they don't yet understand it.* They have, or are cultivating, the belief and certainty that life is always working for them and understand that this is one of the most important beliefs one can hold. They know and operate from the knowing that there are no mistakes, failures, or coincidences, and they cannot lose at this game. They trust that every soul, God, and the Universe know what they're doing.

- *They understand that as human beings it is not our job to control things, or figure out "the how" in life.* They recognize that our job is to know what we want and feel good as often as possible, elevating our vibration consistently enough to allow the Universe to take care of "the how."

- *They understand that ALL moments of struggle, pain, anxiety, worry, fear, doubt, discomfort, and discontent are caused by where one is currently placing one's attention.* In these moments, they consistently shift their attention to something that feels better, knowing that when they do so they are getting themselves to a more resourceful state.

- *They practice the art of "Get into alignment and then,"* *which means they strive to approach all aspects of their daily lives from a place of alignment.* They have become adept at avoiding thoughts of importance or that are stressful when they are in a vibrationally low place. They recognize that nothing good or productive comes from doing so and simply don't go there, knowing they can come back to it when they are in a better-feeling place.

- *They understand that it is okay to feel negative emotions and think negative thoughts, and that it is far more productive to embrace them rather than attempting to resist them.* They also recognize that the trick is not to stay in the negativity, but to focus their thoughts upwards from there. They process those emotions in a healthy way (e.g., crying, journaling, venting, lying in bed all day, etc.) and after they do so they consciously use their tools to move on and up! They understand and accept that negative thoughts and emotions are a part of being human, and it's important to use them for the purpose in which they were intended rather than being consumed by them.

- *They spend as much time as possible daydreaming, visualizing, imagining, and pretending all of the things their hearts desire!* They keep the focus on the end result, not "the how" of it manifesting.

- *They deeply know and understand that pleasure, play, fun, enjoyment, and feeling good is a top priority, as it is the very vibration that precedes all that one wants to accomplish or "get done."* They are very aware and conscious of what nourishes their soul, and intentionally build everything else around that.

- *They focus on their own well-being and alignment in ALL situations, understanding that when they do so everything else falls into place.* This includes the constant management of their thoughts and emotions, especially when dealing with something challenging, in such a way that restores their feelings of well-being as quickly as possible.

- *They live out loud, meaning they no longer have the tendency to hide their beliefs, preferences, values, and opinions for the sake of making another more comfortable.* In fact, they find it very difficult, if not impossible, to hide who they are.

- *They are self-compassionate, and show kindness to themselves.* Even if they don't feel it right away, they make the effort to get there through such things as positive self-talk and a willingness to see themselves another way.

- *They are able and willing to see the bigger picture and explore other perspectives.* They understand the power of perspective, and that each person is operating from their chosen point of view. They strive to empathize, and understand where the other is coming from, rather than push their own agenda.

- *They understand that life is not meant to be lived from just the soul, just the mind, or just the body, but a combination of all three.* They work to integrate these three components of the Self through conscious awareness and practices of mindfulness.

- *They are comfortable with discomfort, or at least accepting of it as part of the process.* They decide ahead of time to accept and embrace feelings of discomfort, and look to see how they can use them rather than condemning them.

- *They know what their intuition looks and feels like, and use it consciously and with intention.* They understand that feelings are the language of the soul, and therefore pay attention to what they are feeling in any given moment.

- *They find it easy to see the beauty in others and hold all other life forms in high regard, because they have cultivated that love and reverence within themselves first.* They practice the knowing that "ours is not a better way, ours is merely another way."

31

This is not to say that people who live a life of alignment feel this way 100% of the time. I'd imagine if they did they would be dead or non-human. Rather, they have access to this type of living every day, are aware of it, and consciously choose it more often than not. Sure, they still have their fall-down moments and uncomfortable growth spurts; yet they remain connected to the larger picture, the larger purpose, and tend to "bounce back" more easily and perhaps more quickly.

Outside Work Counts, Too

Another commonality amongst those who have experienced a certain measure of being Who They Really Are is that they are very aware of what does and doesn't support their alignment, and act accordingly. I'm referring to things in our physical environment, the external influences we come across on a day-to-day basis that we participate in without necessarily realizing we have a choice in it. Having this awareness makes this whole process so much easier, believe me, because it removes a lot of the effort. When you know something isn't good for you and you choose to simply avoid or eliminate it from your experience, it gives you more energy, space, and time to fill yourself up with the stuff that is good for you, right? Conversely, when you know something makes you really happy and feels really good, it stands to reason that, if you make sure to include a lot of it in your life, it will only support and expand that happiness. It's really about *making the decision ahead of time* to include or not include these external factors in your life.

The "influencers" can be big or small, ranging from where you are choosing to live, who you're choosing to surround yourself with, to what kind of clothes you wear, or even which colors you decorate your house with. I am an ambiance gal, so I am keenly aware of anything that empha-sizes or takes away from that. For example, I intentionally have neutral or warm colors in my home, own all of the modern conveniences possible for making seasonal bever-ages such as an electric tea kettle and a milk-frother, I dif-fuse essential oils on the daily, live in yoga pants 99.9% of the time, and have an app on my phone that plays ocean sounds while I work. To get your brain going on this, here are some other things that really support my alignment:

- Getting ample amounts of solitude and downtime
- Spending quality time with my family each and every day (I am SUPER protective of this one)
- Getting enough sleep
- Drinking nearly a gallon of water each day
- Eating nutritious foods that make me feel good physically
- Moving my body daily, so I joined a gym
- Being around like-minded, positive people
- Getting daily doses of pleasure, play, and fun
- Having one-on-one time with my husband
- Enjoying silence, low, or soothing noise
- Being in or having a view of nature
- Listening to audiobooks
- Laughing, humor, levity, wit, and wisely-used sarcasm

Some things that negatively impact my alignment (i.e., make me want to cry or punch someone in the face) are:

- Reading negative or graphic posts on social media
- Watching the news
- Having too much noise going on at once, or loud noises
- Answering my phone or accepting invites out of obligation

- Not allowing myself enough time to get ready for things
- Wearing uncomfortable clothing
- Being overcommitted
- Engaging in gossip or drama
- Giving too much attention to what others think
- Dealing with crabby, whiny children (can't always avoid this one, unfortunately)
- Having not enough or too much solitude
- Eating too much junk food

I make a conscious effort to avoid or not include any of those things in my daily experience, therefore making it easier for me to feel good and access the higher versions of myself more frequently. If I come across them anyway, which most certainly happens because I do not live in a cave, I am aware that they are triggers and I make a conscious effort to shift my energy and attention appropriately. The goal isn't to completely avoid these things, as contrast is a necessity and a gift, but to bring awareness to our choices and where we are putting our attention. This naturally tips the scales towards ease, flow, and well-being.

The same can be said about the good stuff that supports your alignment. It isn't about obsessively ensuring that it is only sunshine and lollipops in your environment or else you will melt down; it's about consciously placing and including these things in your life more and more so that you are less shakable and can recover more quickly when the unwanted does happen. The more you are consciously choosing to fill your space, time, and energy with things that support your alignment, the more empowered you will feel, and the more congruent and fulfilling of a life you will lead.

Practical Application:

Let's take a moment to identify what does and doesn't support your own alignment and well-being, so you can begin naturally adopting more of the qualities listed above. Do not skip this! It's a simple, proactive thing you can do to make your life a whole heckuva lot easier and enjoyable. Trust me, you'll thank me later. Once you've identified these things, work to intentionally put things into place for yourself.

Take out your journal and make detailed notes about each of the following.

1. Things that support my alignment with Who I Really Am are:

2. Things that do not support my alignment with Who I Really Am are:

To Summarize Alignment...

- Alignment is your access point to being Who You Really Are.
- Being in a state of alignment can be described as "feeling good," or being centered, calm, clear, and connected.
- There are varying degrees of alignment, and how good you are feeling is indicative of how much you are currently in alignment.
- The goal is not necessarily to stay in alignment 100% of the time. The goal is to live a life of alignment most of the time, and know what to do to get back into alignment once you are out of it.
- Contrast, or unwanted experience, plays an important role in alignment and being Who You Really Are. It is what allows us to identify and clearly define who we are and what we want.
- There are endless benefits to focusing on one's own alignment and well-being, but the biggest one is

feeling good. When you are in a state of alignment, you feel really good, which raises your vibration to such a level that things come together easily.

- Those who focus on living a life of alignment share many commonalities, or "symptoms" of alignment. In short, they are happy, flexible, highly adaptive, and embrace what is before them. They are not exempt from having challenging moments or experience, but they do tend to recover from them more quickly, as they remain connected to the "bigger picture," or truth of their being.

- Experiencing alignment with Who You Really Are is largely an inside job; that is, it comes from consistently being keenly aware of and focused on your thoughts, emotions, and energy, and channeling them in the right direction. However, external support structures are very useful in maintaining alignment. Being aware of what does and doesn't support your state of alignment, and acting accordingly with that knowledge, can make a big difference.

- Above all else, awareness and conscious intentions are key to living a life of alignment. By being aware of what honestly feels good to you, and making feeling good your highest priority, you will achieve a life of alignment with Who You Really Are.

PART 2:
EMBRACING YOUR HUMANITY

This section covers the topic of being human, and how to embrace that as part of the perfection of Who You Really Are, rather than seeing this tiny detail as a flaw or an imperfection. From the stories of Adam and Eve to the various perspectives and belief systems religions and cultures hold, we've been told that simply by being what we are–human–we are already damaged goods. Furthermore, we are encouraged to spend our lives not only apologizing for this, but also striving to somehow denounce or rise above it. I'll be blunt: that's insanity.

I really want you to get that becoming more "evolved," "enlightened," "spiritually aware," or "aligned with Who You Really Are" does not in any way, shape, or form mean you stop being human. On the contrary, it allows you to embrace your humanity, which is an extremely important piece to merging your spirituality with your humanity and being Who You Really Are. I have noticed that many of the resources in the spiritual/self-development community paint a picture of the impossible goal of being "perfect" and exclude the many aspects of life that tend to kick us around a bit, such as caring what others think of us or making mistakes. I strongly feel this is a huge disservice to those who are seeking to know, understand, and become more. After all, we are not only "spiritual beings having a human experience," we are also "human beings having a spiritual experience." I deeply want you to not only learn how to enjoy your humanity on a whole new level of pleasure, fun, and acceptance, but to learn that it's okay to be human in the first place. Dropping the resistance to being human opens the doorway for so much more love and possibility.

I'm going to offer you some different ideas, as well as ways to apply them, that move you away from these old, broken systems of thinking and living and towards a life of embracing and being Who You Really Are. Of course, I encourage you to decide if these concepts are valuable to you or not, and act accordingly. That's part of the beauty of being human. We get to decide for ourselves.

Chapter 4
Being Human is Okay, Too, Ya Know

"Your authenticity is mesmerizing, your vulnerability is captivating, your flaws are enchanting, your light is breathtaking, your love is spellbinding. You are magic."
~ *Creig Crippen*

I don't know where being human became such a bad thing. Have you ever noticed that we often find ourselves even apologizing for it? "Sorry, I'm human," we say, after we've made a mistake or unintentionally offended someone. "You're only human" is what we hear when we've realized we've reached our limit in what we can accomplish in a day or in what we can juggle at once. It's offered as an excuse or a way out, yet simultaneously, and perhaps unconsciously, condemning us for such a condition.

With the explosion of awakenings and shifts in consciousness, that have especially occurred in the last decade, has come the assumption that now that we are awake, we must strive to be positive and spiritual all the time. I don't know that anyone actually says that, but it's definitely out there, and it doesn't exactly leave a lot of room to be human.

Being human is not a "condition" that goes away once you become spiritual. Yet, I see this unspoken belief all the time in my work as a spiritual coach. The relief my clients feel is palpable in the moment they realize that it's okay to not be "Mother Theresa" all the time. It is in that very moment of reckoning that the merging of their spirituality with their humanity takes a huge leap forward.

I had my "moment" right around the time *The Secret* catapulted the Law of Attraction into a mainstream concept. Having already been immersed in the spiritual development community for a while I saw many others rise with excitement right along with me at the concepts being offered, and fall flat on their faces with me, countless times, in the attempt to practically apply them. We were under the assumption that in order to successfully use the Law of Attraction to your benefit, *you must be positive. All. The. Time.*

I realized quickly this was not feasible.

What's that? You're having a negative thought? Quick, get rid of it!! You don't like that experience? Don't you dare admit it! Smile and say something positive, quick! Don't you know the Law of Attraction is *watching*??? Being that we are indeed human, and inevitably encounter negative thoughts and experiences daily, this approach is certainly not sustainable.

In the moment that we were given, perhaps, our greatest freedom–the knowing of ourselves as the consciously creative beings that we all are–we simultaneously began dancing with a very subtle, yet powerful, pressure to cease being human. In fact, the stakes were raised now because, given the power of our thoughts, being human was a huge obstacle to manifesting all those cars, houses, dream jobs, and soul mates we desired.

There just wasn't a lot of talk about what to do with that very human side of ourselves while attempting to be more of our spiritual, aware, conscious, and creative selves. It was almost dismissed, as if it would no longer be an issue if you could just make sure that all 60,000+ thoughts you had a day were positive ones. If you've met someone who has managed to accomplish this, by the way, please introduce me. I would love to meet her or him!

As I was working very hard to think positively all the freakin' time, while silently condemning myself for those moments that it just wasn't happening, I actually found myself in a state of resistance more than ever before.

I became increasingly frustrated with the process, because I deeply believed the Law of Attraction to be true, but couldn't seem to get it right. I was trying to consciously use the process to create tangible success in my coaching business. I was just starting out, doing great work with the clients I did have but there weren't too many of those, and my income was next to nothing. I remember the struggle and confusion of knowing I was on the right path, yet feeling there was something I was missing. This missing piece was the very thing that had me repeating the experience of "failure."

I took a break from the Law of Attraction at that point, which is funny because that's just impossible. It's happening with or without our conscious awareness. But in my mind, it was more of a, "Screw it, I give up for now, I'll just roll with It" sort of thing. It wasn't actually until a few years later that I found that missing piece: *being human is not an obstacle in the game of conscious creation; it is an asset when embraced, understood, and used properly.*

Like so many others, I had been unconsciously, and oftentimes quite consciously, condemning my humanness; such as my tendency to think negative thoughts, feel negative emotions, and act in ways that were not in alignment with who I wanted to be. I was trying to eradicate my humanness, so to speak, in my attempt to be more of my spiritual self. I didn't understand that my human self was a part of my spiritual self, and that it is a very necessary and useful component in experiencing Who I Really Am.

This new understanding emerged when I began consciously and consistently engaging in habits and practices that supported my alignment. In fact, it was early in my coaching with Dustin where he had me fill out a worksheet that asked some in-depth questions about who I am and who I wanted to be.

When I was noting some of the things I liked the most about myself, I noticed that they were very human characteristics instead of what you would typically describe as spiritual ones:

- My well-used sarcasm, wit, and humor,
- Being a smart ass,
- Swearing,
- Occasional irreverence,
- My love of the Simpsons,
- The extreme joy and pleasure I've always taken in playing hooky,
- My love of doing nothing,
- and other similar attributes.

Then Dustin asked me what it would be like if I could be those aspects of myself *while* I was deeply impacting the lives of others. What if it could be that fun and effortless? He then asked me the extremely powerful question, "What if being exactly and authentically who you are was the key to the success you desire?"

I had to sit with that one for a bit because I knew that question touched on something hugely important. I couldn't yet name it, but I felt a physical response upon hearing it, the kind you feel when you know you've heard a Truth.

I journaled and meditated on this question for quite some time and I determined that living in alignment with Who You Really Are includes those very human parts of you.

If you were to deny those parts of yourself, as in, simply pretend they weren't there, including all of the negative thoughts and emotions, mistakes made, and the vulnerability felt, you would be shutting the door to all that you were trying to allow in. It finally clicked that when you do so, it is impossible to experience alignment with Who You Really Are.

From that moment on I made it my business to practice embracing the parts of me that I had previously decided, for one reason or another, weren't spiritual enough. I decided to take pleasure in them, too. What that looked like for me was no longer filtering my words when working with my clients or when interacting with loved ones. I no longer adapted to their language, for the sake of their comfort, and to the detriment of mine. It looked like not trying so damned hard to get it right, or to appear like I had my shit together all the time. And it looked like embracing my negative thoughts and emotions, instead of condemning myself for having them in the first place.

Living in alignment was absolutely liberating, and the more I consciously focused on it, the easier it was to do. As a result, I began attracting more of my ideal clients who, wouldn't you know it?, wanted to pay me my full rates! And, in return, I had an absolute blast serving them because it felt like just being myself.

You Know You're Human When...

I'd like to get a bit more specific about what it means to be human. I find, when you look at it kind of big-picture style, and know that it pertains to literally every other person on this planet, it's easier to embrace those parts within yourself. Embracing has a diffusing (or releasing) energy to it, too, by the way. That's why embracing your human side is such an important element to merging your humanity with your spirituality. All that time spent resisting our human selves results in the build up of a tremendous amount of pressure and energy that block us in so many ways and block us from seeing so many truths. The second we move from resistance into surrender and then to embracing, we oftentimes feel immediate relief because that intense energy is instantly diffused. The energy lightens, and space is created for new, more desirable things to fill it.

Let's shine the light on some things about being human, and as you read below and acknowledge these within yourself, notice how it feels to know that everyone else has these traits too. Just for funsies, we're going to go kind of "You know you're a redneck when" style here....

You Know You're a Human when you:

- Feel vulnerable sometimes
- Have an ego and use it
- Care what others think (don't even try to deny this one)
- Make mistakes
- Have emotions
- Are self-centered at times, okay most of the time, even when you think you aren't
- Have wants, desires, needs, and preferences
- Don't get it right all the time
- Feel immense amounts of pain
- Feel immense amounts of love
- Feel emotions you can't even name
- Get stressed and overwhelmed

- Have a tendency to react and overreact
- Feel empathy and compassion
- Have an imagination
- Are resourceful
- Have the ability to take on different perspectives
- Sometimes feel as though life is working against you
- Sometimes feel as if you are alone
- Sometimes compare yourself to others
- Sometimes laugh and cry in the same day, or even in the same minute
- Have felt shame or guilt
- Desire human touch and affection
- Seek connection, love, and growth
- Are constantly changing or encountering change
- Have a sense of value and contribution
- Have gifts and talents as well as weaknesses and vulnerabilities
- Sometimes feel as if no one else can possibly understand what you are going through
- Learn through living, even though sometimes you expect or are expected to know better
- Crave certainty, yet also enjoy variety
- Yearn to feel significant and connected

What did you notice as you read this list? Where did your heart sink and where did it rise? Did you notice that there is plenty of diversity to this list, plenty of things you might label "good" and "bad?" That's because we are beings of duality, of light and dark, so to speak. We have the dark aspects in order to bring out, and experience, the light aspects. In other words, you can't know yourself as strong unless you've experienced, and known yourself, as weak, as discussed earlier. Since those "bad" aspects serve such a great purpose, why on earth would we want to condemn them? And how is it serving us to resist or condemn aspects of ourselves that we all share, that no one is exempt from? It simply isn't. Resisting and condemning our humanness are the very things that create such dysfunction in our lives and in society. Furthermore, resisting and condemning parts of ourselves, that are present because they have a function and a purpose, feels bad. It's simple: when we feel negative, we do "bad" things, or things that are not in alignment with Who We Really Are.

What if you knew that it's okay to be all that is listed above at different moments in your life, and that they are necessary parts of the equation that is both the human AND the spiritual experience? What might happen if you could allow your mind to relax in the endless pursuit of condemning or resisting any of it? What other more desirable experiences would you then make room for? Where else could you use that energy? I invite you to try the embracing route and see for yourself.

Practical Application:

Take out your journal and write down all of the aspects of your "human self" that you like, enjoy, and love. Allow yourself to feel good about them as you do so.

When you can't think of anymore, write down all of your "human self" aspects that are *difficult* for you to like, enjoy, or love. For each one, look for something to appreciate about it, and write that down next to it. For example, if you don't enjoy the fact that you are dependent on others for certain things, perhaps you can appreciate that you have others to turn to at all.

CHAPTER 5
MY EGO MADE ME DO IT

*"If you deny your ego, it will push back against you harder.
The more you reject something, the more it fights back for its
own survival. But when you can completely love your ego
unconditionally and accept it as part of how you express in
this life, you'll no longer have a problem with it."*

~ *Anita Moorjani*

I'd like to talk a little bit about one aspect of being human
that I, and others, think gets an unfair, bad rap: the ego. I
am by no means an expert in this subject; I only have my own
experience, observations, and musings to offer you here. At
the risk of being called out by ego experts, I'm going to go
out on a limb and say I am not convinced the ego is such a
bad thing. In fact, I will even go so far as to say that I like and
appreciate my ego (gasp!).

Remember a moment ago when I said that the less desirable parts of being human have a purpose and serve a specific function? The ego is included in that. The ego actually
has a starring role in this production of Being Who You
Really Are; it's like that character you love to hate, or know
you should hate but you actually really love.

The ego is described in many ways, depending on the context, but in the spiritual development world it has been described as "your smaller self" or the part of you that is disconnected or separate, the part that gets you in trouble or off your path. I'm not saying that all of the spiritual teachers who speak on this topic are wrong, and I certainly don't want to start a debate about what exactly the ego is. I more so want to shed light on the parts that I believe may be misinterpreted by many, including myself at one time, and are causing a disconnect from Who We Really Are.

I have, all too often, come across this misinterpretation of the ego while working with my clients. Somewhere along the way they "learned" that the ego is bad and we should run for the hills from it or squash it out, rather than trying to understand and use it for the purpose in which it was intended. I've noticed that whole purpose part tends to get skipped over frequently, and I'm guessing it's a huge piece of missing information that causes misinterpretation in the first place.

I have a hunch that, because the ego is looked at in a more negative light, it is an area that causes the most resistance and condemnation within oneself. For research purposes, I polled a bunch of people through social media to see what different understandings of the ego were out there. I was curious to see if it lined up with what I had been observing for years with my clients and like-minded friends: That the ego is a "bad" part of us that we should seek to "overcome." Sure enough, that was the overall tone of the responses I received. In general, people feel bad about having an ego, despite seeming to understand that it plays a part in identifying who they are.

I know that every time I read or hear about the ego described as a part of us that needs to be overcome or ignored, it makes me feel bad, which is my indication from my soul that I'm not in alignment with whatever it is I am focusing on. It doesn't make sense to me. How could that be true if it is also widely said that we are the yin and the yang, the light and the dark, and are whole beings? Why would God make an inherent part of us "bad?"

Eckhart Tolle describes the ego as being a representation of our thoughts, how we tend to identify ourselves through them, and that the quality of our thoughts therefore matters. He says that "you derive your sense of who you are from what your mind is telling you about who you are." Following that logic, if your mind is constantly playing the track of "I am not enough," then that is how your ego will help you identify yourself. However, if your mind happens to play the track of "I am more than enough," well, then that's a different story.

I look at the ego as a neutral vehicle. It will respond and "guide" based on the quality of our thoughts. It is there as a mechanism for us to choose Who We Are, and it is one of life's many tools of opportunity. The key to using it for our highest good is vigilant self-awareness and the willingness to choose the highest thoughts, words, and deeds available.

Abraham-Hicks talks about the ego as your "point of focus," stating that ego is "awareness of the self and caring how the self feels." If you're aware of the teachings of Abraham-Hicks then you know they strongly emphasize that how you feel in any given moment is the most important thing, considering that feelings determine our vibration and keeping our vibration high is what keeps us in a state of allowing. Regarding the purpose of the ego, they say, "We don't want to omit the ego, we just want to train it into alignment."

Neale Donald Walsch says, "The ego that's run amuck is not okay, but ego at its basis has really gotten a bad rap. If you don't know Who You Are, you will have no idea what you are trying to achieve in your life."

And Wayne Dyer says, "The ego part of you is nothing more than the action of your beliefs."

As you can see, there is nothing inherently negative or bad about the ego itself. What's important is how we choose to use it in our lives, and whether or not we are doing a good job keeping it in balance with our spirit. Like all things that exist, both the light and the dark and the yin and the yang, the ego is yet another aspect of God. We just need to strive not to Edge God Out (E.G.O.) as we move about our lives.

For example, I am very clear that the majority of the material in this book is coming *through* me rather than *from* me. In fact, anytime I engage in a coaching session with a client I am clear as day that all I have to do is show up and allow the Universe, my guides, the client's guides, God, or whatever you want to label it, to work through me. This fact would not be obvious to someone if they happened to be listening in, however, nor is it obvious to those reading this book. Why? Because my ego is the thing that allows the info flowing through me to be delivered in a specific way, namely through my personality and style of writing. In other words, the "filter" the Universe is working through is, essentially, my ego, or my identity. This includes my perspectives, opinions, and experience.

Throughout this writing process, I have had to do some major self-management when it comes to being careful not to *edge God out*. I am careful not to write unless I am in a state of alignment and am feeling good, and if I'm not, I practice backing off until I can get my vibration raised again. Otherwise, I am looking at the possibility of letting my ego take over and losing that precious balance.

As I mentioned above, balancing the ego with the spirit requires self-awareness and willingness, mostly in the form of *emotional and thought management*. Another way of referring to this is "vibrational management," as our thoughts and emotions are what determine our vibration in any given moment. This involves paying attention to the way we feel, identifying the thoughts that are causing us to feel that way, and making any necessary adjustments to get to an aligned, good-feeling place. All of the exercises in this book are examples of ways to do this, actually, including the one I am about to share with you below.

What does that mean for you? First off, more embracing, my friend. Make peace with the fact that you have an ego and that it is an asset, not a detriment, to becoming more of Who You Really Are. Seek not to extinguish its voice, but to embrace and integrate it in a way that contributes to the whole. What this may look like for you is to get really good at noticing which voice is speaking on your behalf at any given moment: is it your mind/ego, your body, or your soul? And once you've determined which, ask yourself if what it is saying is serving you. If it isn't, look to what it is showing you about yourself, and ask yourself what might serve you instead.

That's really my point here, to ease some more of the resistance that lives in you, and that lives in me. To give us all permission to stop with the condemnation that has us running in circles instead of moving forward with grace, awareness, and intention. *All parts of us are good parts, and all play a vital role.* But how do you practically do that in everyday life moments? Well, being a practical application gal, I have discovered something that works for me in this department. I have outlined my favorite go-to move for embracing

any kind of ego-based thought or experience below, for you
to try yourself.

Practical Application:

Any time you notice yourself feeling an emotion that doesn't
feel good, if you pause long enough you can usually trace
it back to a thought that caused the feeling. If the thought
doesn't make you feel good, you can bet that it is not representative of your highest truth about that given thing. It
is most likely based in fear or "old data," which is coming
from your ego. Instead of feeling worse about identifying
your ego as the culprit, quietly thank your ego for being the
way-shower of what doesn't match Who You Really Are. It is
simply doing its job.

Then, take the thought that doesn't feel good and see
what you can appreciate about it. As thoughts can sometimes be messy, I like to use the following structure: "Even
though I feel _____, I appreciate _____."

For example: "Even though I am angry at myself for
not being prepared and I am tempted to berate myself for
it, I appreciate that I usually am prepared and this feeling
reminds me of how important that is to me."

By acknowledging and embracing the negative feeling
you are having, you are creating a sense of relief within
yourself that allows you to move into appreciation. By noticing that there is something to appreciate even within this
unpleasant feeling you are experiencing, even more relief
is created. The energy of appreciation is a great neutralizer
and gently assists us into higher thoughts and vibrations,
and naming the negative thoughts and emotions helps you
to embrace the role your ego is playing. Used together in
this way, they both allow you to move up the emotional/
vibrational scale much more quickly and easily.

CHAPTER 6
IF IT'S THERE, IT'S SUPPOSED TO BE

"Accept—then act. Whatever the present moment contains, accept it as if you had chosen it. Always work with it, not against it...This will miraculously transform your whole life."

~ Eckhart Tolle

Speaking of embracing, this is a good time to talk about the concept of "embracing what is." As stated earlier, I believe the majority of individual suffering that takes place is due to resisting "what is." In other words, we tend to put most, if not all, of our energy into insisting that what is showing up in our lives shouldn't be there. In the insistence that it shouldn't be there we are unconsciously denying the very truth of our being: that we are conscious co-creators here on this earth to declare and define, express and experience—Who We Really Are. This is done through the endless combinations of factors, aspects, elements, and resources this world provides us. Denial of this truth, and denial that what is currently present in our lives is indeed there to serve us, even if it doesn't look like it at first, causes pain and suffering when it is meant to provide an experience of the joy of expansion.

Through my work as a coach, as well as the go-to person for friends and family members when life throws a curve ball, I have observed that enormous amounts of time and energy are wasted in the realm of "it shouldn't be this way" or "I didn't want this." While I get it, and have certainly done my fair share of this myself throughout my life, I can't deny the vibrational mechanics that take place when this happens.

It works like this: During the time that we are spending focused on what shouldn't be, we are in a state of resistance; we are practicing a consistently low vibration that doesn't allow us access to the things we want and Who We Want To Be. By condemning what is before us we are blocking the very experiences of joy, love, peace, and freedom that we desire. We continue to "beat the drum" of what shouldn't be, getting stuck in story mode. We play it over and over again, re-telling our story of what is wrong or bad to anyone who will listen. If this pattern doesn't get interrupted either intentionally or unintentionally, it can lead to even deeper suffering such as chronic depression or anxiety. Through our vibration, it also sends a message to the Universe to send us more experiences and contexts like it, even though we are certain we don't want them!

Interrupting this pattern forever can be done by adopting one of the most important beliefs and practices I believe there is: Embracing What Is. This belief says that when something seemingly unwanted shows up in our experience, strive to embrace and accept it as somehow supporting and moving us forward on our path. We don't have to like it and we don't have to understand it—most of the time we won't initially. But if we can make peace with its presence and accept that it is somehow serving our highest good, as well as that of everyone else's, we will give ourselves tremendous freedom, relief, and spaciousness. We also position ourselves to be resourceful, conscious, and intentional with what happens next, not to mention moving into receiving mode or a state of allowing.

And here's the thing, even if this is complete B.S., there is still a high amount of functional value offered in this practice. Think about the last time you felt really beaten down by something that happened. How capable did you feel to handle it? Did you even have a desire to? I'm guessing not, and I'm also guessing that you spent more time than you would have preferred to, swirling in the overall suckiness of it all before you eventually picked yourself back up and moved forward. Throughout that time, you were in a lower state of being and had limited access to what you needed to thrive. Your brain and body probably weren't working as highly as they could have been. In fact, if the situation was really unpleasant, it probably negatively impacted some other areas of your life as well.

Now imagine that instead of spending all that time and energy swirling in the lower, limited-access emotional states, you had responded by embracing what happened and accepting that it was serving a higher purpose, one you simply couldn't identify yet. What might be different? I'm guessing overall the experience would have been shorter, easier to deal with, and you would have found yourself to be more resourceful. Do you see the value in that?

My client, Deana, who is now one of my trained Spiritual Alignment Coaches, used this belief in a difficult situation beautifully and even better than I had anticipated she would. The biggest desire she had was to leave her corporate job and corporate life of ten years, identify her life's purpose, and move into a career that matched it. Well, being the incredibly supportive Universe that It is, just a few weeks into our work together Deana was let go at her corporate job. She emailed me for an "emergency session" when this happened, and being that we were just a few weeks into our coaching journey together I was sure I was going to have to talk her off a ledge (not literally) and walk her through the panic, anxiety, and overall resistance to what was happening. She surprised the heck out of me when I answered the phone and her voice actually sounded chipper! In fact, her entire energy was different, lighter, as if a weight had been lifted. Instead of helping her to process her emotions before moving her in the direction her soul so clearly wanted to go, we had a fantastic session revolving around how much in awe she was of the Universe stepping in on her behalf.

You see, she already had the basis of the belief of "embracing what is" in place, and she got to act on it consciously in a safe, supportive environment (our coaching). The best part was she had no idea what she was going to do next, but she didn't feel fear around it, at least not yet. Deana was consciously choosing to see what was occurring as a gift, and trusting that although there was a lot she didn't yet know or understand, the Universe had her back. This gave her such freedom and reassurance, especially in the weeks to come, when the fear inevitably did creep in. She is now in the process of creating a wonderfully fulfilling and impactful, spiritually based, entrepreneurial career, and she is no longer "slowly dying inside," as she had put it.

Another place this belief really comes in handy is in grief and loss, and having experienced it firsthand a few times myself, I bet there are a lot of you whose muscles just contracted at those words. But hear me out—I'm not saying it's easy, I'm saying it is really useful. I find that losing someone or something immeasurably important to you is perhaps the largest and loudest context there is of "this shouldn't have happened" and is arguably the most difficult to navigate.

When my dad passed away at 62-years-old from a fifteen-year battle with cancer, this belief saved me. His passing was just under two years ago at the time I am writing this, and I had been cultivating this belief that life is always working for us consciously for almost two decades, so it was already strongly in place when this most painful of events occurred. I distinctly remember the phone call from my mom while I was sitting on the couch breastfeeding my, not even, two-month-old, informing me that they were just told there was nothing more they could do for my dad and he had chosen to finish out his days in home hospice care. This was not an "embracing" moment for me. I shattered and crumbled into a million tiny pieces in that instant. I think I even began yelling "no" as I was crying and breaking down, tears falling on my daughter. I was resisting what was and it was, hands-down, one of the most painful moments of my life, in every sense of the word, as it should have been.

This is one of the few types of instances where I wouldn't recommend moving straight into embracing mode. I'm not even sure it's humanly possible. I guess in a way I was embracing, however, because I was embracing the pain. I could've very well just shut down and repressed the hell out of it, but for me that wasn't an option, and in retrospect I am grateful for that.

In the moments, days, and weeks that followed, it was an indescribably horrific experience of watching someone I loved and adored beyond words drift away, deteriorate, and suffer right before my eyes. I did my very best to care for him, care for my two young children, and support my mom all while feeling absolutely helpless inside, nearing a mental and physical breakdown on more than one occasion. Then there was the moment of his physical departure, the intense and illogical mix of emotions that followed, and attempting to piece life together again while integrating his physical absence. Throughout all of that, this belief was indeed my saving grace. Had I not had that underlying peace of knowing that this, too, was somehow serving the higher purpose of all, I am certain I would have ended up in the hospital myself at some point, and moving forward with my life would have felt impossible.

Each tiny step of the way, I consciously *and* unconsciously reminded myself that all was in divine, perfect order, even if I didn't see or understand it yet. More importantly, that I was completely loved and held by God and by Life itself. I can never accurately convey how much comfort and love this belief and practice gave me during that time.

It allowed me to grasp and understand that my dad's soul chose to depart at that time and in the manner it did for countless higher reasons and benefits, many of which I have been able to identify bit by bit over the past couple of years, and I feel an enormous amount of gratitude for that. I don't ask you to share that particular perspective, I get that it's a lot. But if it rings true to you on any level, I highly recommend the book *Home with God* by Neale Donald Walsch, which goes into a deeper explanation of death.

Embracing what is does not mean that you are giving up, that you have no say in what is happening next. It means quite the opposite. It is a belief and a practice that invites you to connect with and participate in your life, *in all of Life*, more deeply than perhaps you thought possible. It places you in the driver's seat of creation, the seat you were meant and always invited to sit in. It invites flow and eases resistance. It cultivates trust and certainty. If it feels like a stretch for you even after reading these words, then I invite you to at least move into the space of willingness. Be willing to adopt this belief and practice. It is one of the most loving things you can do for yourself.

Practical Application

I am going to borrow this tool from the very person who gave me this belief in the first place. It's more of a prayer, or mantra, if you like, for those moments where you are faced with something unpleasant in life that you are certain you didn't call forth. You can read more about it in Neale Donald Walsch's book, *Happier Than God.*

When faced with these life events and experiences, and the thoughts and emotions that come with them, pause long enough to say, *"Thank you God/Universe, for the gift in this experience, even if I don't know what it is yet."* Or any version of that. This acts as an anchor, or an active reminder of this truth that life and God are always working for us, even when it does not appear to be so. It also provides a measure of instant relief, which is sometimes all you need to feel in order to take that next positive step forward. I recommend writing this prayer, or one similar to it, on a notecard and either posting it somewhere visible or carrying it around with you until it becomes habit.

You may also want to take out your journal and identify at least one area, aspect, or circumstance in your life currently that you find yourself resisting. Then, underneath it, write out the above mantra. This makes the choosing of this belief more *real* in your mind, and helps you more easily line up your behavior with it.

Chapter 7
Negative Thoughts
are Not Your Enemy

"Everything contains a special purpose and a hidden message."

~ Marcus Aurelius

Just as "embracing what is" allows you to access your most resourceful self and your next steps forward more quickly and smoothly, embracing your negative thoughts and emotions has a similar effect. I'm going to go much further in-depth with how to do this in very functional ways, but what I want you to know about it right now is that your negative thoughts, emotions, and experiences are a gift.

Yes, you read that right. They are a gift and you can be happy that you have them and will continue to have them for the rest of your life. In fact, humor me and pause for a moment to take that in. *You will have negative thoughts, emotions, and experiences for the rest of your life.* In this moment you are invited to acknowledge, embrace, and accept this, because when you do, you relieve yourself of the pressure and the false truth that the goal is to *stop having them*. Doesn't that feel better, knowing that you don't have to accomplish the impossible?

Negativity is a gift because it serves a purpose...several purposes, in fact. Here are a few:

- *Negativity gives us important information.* In the moment you are having a negative thought, emotion, or experience, you are very aware of what you don't want. Simultaneously, you are gifted with clarity on what you *do* want, which is a vital thing to know in terms of conscious creation. There is never an instance where this isn't true. Go ahead, try it now. Conjure up a negative thought you have or have had, and take a look at what it's showing you about what you want. For example, if you're having the negative thought, "Everything bad happens to me," then you know instantly that you want everything that happens to you to be "good."

- *Negativity helps us define who we are.* Much like the first bullet point, negativity of any kind gives us information about who we are and who we want to be, where we are and where we are going, and strongly contributes to the conscious defining and expressing of that. In the moment we experience ourselves as something we aren't, we become crystal clear about who we are or who we want to be.

- *Negativity helps us process our energy.* As human beings, we often bottle things up, suppress and repress emotions, hide from ourselves, and hide ourselves from others. This can create a disconnect from Who We Really Are and the connection we feel to life and the world around us, not to mention lead to physical and mental health issues. When we use negativity for the purpose for which it is intended, we are allowing that energy to get processed, provide the gifts it is wanting to, and get funneled up and out of us to provide space for more of the good stuff.

- *Negativity can lead us to our biggest growth.* Oftentimes it is in the moments of our greatest darkness that we encounter our greatest light. We can't know ourselves as strong until we have been weak, or know ourselves as empowered unless we have experienced what it is like to feel helpless. Ignore the negative thoughts and emotions that are accompanying any particular experience and you may be avoiding an opportunity for huge growth.

If you simply try to think positively *all* the time, it is inevitable that you will encounter resistance at some point, especially if you are just plain ignoring your negative thoughts and feelings. First off, what you resist persists. Second, you are human. Remember, on average we have over 60,000 thoughts in a day–you can bet your bottom dollar that a lot of those are going to be less than pleasant and love-based. Instead of trying to force them away or make the fruitless attempt of monitoring every God-blessed one of them, it is far more effective to try managing and directing them in a way that serves you instead.

So how might one do that? By embracing, feeling, acknowledging, and even perhaps indulging in them a bit. Don't worry about what you'll attract by doing this; remember that the trick is not to stay in the negative feeling too long. After processing what you're thinking and feeling, give that energy a safe place to go and shift your attention to something that feels better. For example, you can write it all out in your journal, vent to a trusted friend, or my personal favorite, yell out loud to yourself and throw a fit (what I like to refer to as a "spiritual tantrum"). Then go for a walk, take a nap, eat ice cream, meditate, watch a good movie, exercise, or do something fun. In other words, follow with what feels good and get that vibration up again!

But here's the most important part: *Once you have processed the negative thoughts and emotions, leave them there.* Don't keep telling the same story over and over again. If you do, it is then that you can worry about what you are attracting, which will be more of the same.

I love watching the light bulbs turn on when I inevitably encounter this subject with my clients. I remember one client in particular, we'll call her Christina, being ultra-resistant to engaging in her negative thoughts. Anytime she would tell me something that would surely upset anyone, including myself, she would add, "But on the bright side..." or "But I am grateful for..." This isn't a bad thing at all, of course. Looking for the gift or something to appreciate within a tough situation is a fantastically useful technique, one that I use a lot, as you'll recall from the practical application in chapter five. But what I was seeing with Christina was a sort of tightness in her energy; I could tell it didn't *feel good* for her to say that, despite the cheery demeanor that implied otherwise.

In one instance, I called her out on it, asking "Really? Is it really okay with you that your friend dumped on you like that and treated you so poorly?" She was silent for a moment and then responded quietly, "No, no I guess it isn't." I asked her why she didn't just admit that in the first place, and she said, "Because I don't want the Law of Attraction to bring me more experiences like it." And there it is right there, folks, what I was referring to earlier! The whole think-positively-all-the-time-or-else vibe that came with the release of that popular movie and book. This was the part that didn't get explored or acknowledged, and yet it is so very important.

I had to laugh, remembering a time when I felt the very same thing, and said, "Oh, Christina. I am so, so happy to be able to tell you that it's okay to feel bad sometimes. In fact, it is a necessary part of the equation." We proceeded to have a fantastic discussion about this concept, covering all of the above, and emphasizing that it's very okay to embrace and move through your negative thoughts and emotions from an unpleasant event or experience. I assured her that it's wonderfully human of her to do so and she will not be "punished" by the Law of Attraction or anything else. You can imagine her relief upon hearing this.

I can't say this enough: The trick is to not stay there, but instead consciously choose to go up, meaning shift your focus to something that feels better, and start telling a new story about that thing that upset you. Don't keep repeating it. Decide that your feelings are important, and remember that feeling good is your access point to everything you desire to experience.

Again, we are spiritual beings having a human experience. It is VERY okay to be human, just try to do it consciously and with as much awareness as possible. As I covered in the previous chapter, the quickest way to move out of a state of resistance is to embrace what is showing up, no matter what it looks like. You can do this by reminding yourself that everything you see in your world serves a higher purpose; even the bad things aren't really bad. Embracing what shows up and using it (i.e., deciding who you want to be in light of it) is the smoothest path I know of to getting into that lovely, oh-so-enjoyable state of alignment.

Practical Application

Take a moment to consciously decide ahead of time how you would like to intentionally embrace and process the very natural negative human thoughts and emotions you will continue to encounter in life. In your journal, or on a separate piece of paper that you can post somewhere you will see often, list these "strategies." They may or may not include journaling, crying, venting, screaming out loud, punching your pillow, exercising, or talking it out with a trusted friend or coach. Remind yourself in your writing to choose to go up when you are done, and even identify the strategies you have for that as well. It might look something like this:

From here on out, whenever I find myself having a negative reaction, or negative thoughts and emotions, I will...

After I have embraced and processed my human emotions, I will choose to "go up" by...

Chapter 8

When All of the
Sudden Life Sucks

"Something very beautiful happens to people when their world has fallen apart: a humility, a nobility, a higher intelligence emerges at just the point when our knees hit the floor."

~ *Marianne Williamson*

Navigating your negative thoughts and emotions the way I have described in chapter seven will help you get to a better-feeling state of alignment every time, if you do the work consciously. However, there are moments in life where, despite your best efforts in thought and emotional management, life all of the sudden sucks.

You know what I mean. Life is going along swimmingly and you're in your groove, focused on gratitude and the good stuff most of the time, enjoying the flow. And then shit hits the fan. Things begin to go "wrong," unexpected and often quite intense challenges arise, life feels hard, and you're not quite sure why or how this happened. I mean you're a spiritually aware, conscious co-creator who is doing his/her work, so what the hell is going on?

Sound familiar?

Most people interpret these times as "bad luck," life giving you a swift kick in the rear, or even assume they are doing something wrong. *What is actually happening is a phenomenon often referred to as "The Breakdown before the Breakthrough," a "System Upgrade," or a "Spiritual Upgrade," where you are energetically and neurologically being taken apart and broken down, in order to be put back together in a higher-functioning way.*

I liken it to an engineer taking apart a computer or a machine so that she can add in some new parts, take out some old ones that are no longer needed, and put it all back together in a way that makes it function more efficiently and is easier to use. During the time she has the machine apart in all of its pieces, it looks like a mess and doesn't appear to make sense. This is the breakdown part of the experience, and it can feel like your life has "fallen to pieces" or you may refer to yourself as a "mess."

It is my experience that growth in the areas of consciousness, awareness, and understanding tends to come in levels or phases, because there is only so much we can handle or take on all at once. Think about it: If God appeared before you in this very instant and not only told you everything there was to possibly know about life, being human, and everything beyond, but also gave you all the tools you needed right then and there, what do you think would happen next? You'd likely freeze, overwhelmed by what you had been given because you weren't yet ready for all of it. I always tell my clients that their heads would explode if I gave them everything all at once, and that's why God doesn't give everything to us all at once, either.

Instead, *I believe God has designed an incredible "growth system" whereby we grow in levels, and once we've reached the upper limit or ceiling of a level, we are broken down and rebuilt in order to be capable of experiencing and handling the next.* This way, we are able to explore, experience, and soak in all that we can (or that our souls desire to) at each level, and go about our lives at a much more comfortable and satisfying pace, if you will. When we are ready for more, we know it. How many levels there are, or whether they are in a particular order or not, I have no idea; I guess I'm not at that level of knowing and awareness yet!

I had a client named Suri who was extremely eager and excited when we began our six-month Spiritual Alignment Coaching journey together. The package she purchased included unlimited email support, which I encourage my clients to take full advantage of. I didn't need to tell her twice! Suri was emailing me at least once, sometimes several times each day with questions and queries that weren't even related to what we were currently coaching on. She wanted to know everything there was to know about Spiritual Alignment, about life and the Universe, and she wanted to know it *now.* In one of our earliest calls I took some time to talk about how we grow at exactly the rate we need to, and that it's actually impossible to rush anything. I encouraged her instead to stay focused on the things we were working on currently, and to do her best not to try and jump ahead. She reluctantly agreed.

Only a few weeks into our work together Suri experienced her first (with me) Breakdown before the Breakthrough. She had hit her "upper limit" of the level she was in so quickly. Typically, I didn't have to cover this concept with my clients until nearly halfway through the coaching! I had to laugh, as her eagerness and enthusiasm for this way of living and being were so strong that having a system upgrade so soon shouldn't have surprised me. We worked through it together, and it was then that she began to really understand what I had been talking about.

How it Happens

The Breakdown before the Breakthrough is often signaled by disruptions in your world, or an unusual amount of internal and external challenges. It is different from those times you feel like you are just having a bad day, or you find yourself in a less than pleasant mood. When it's the latter, you can shift yourself out of it using a number of different tools and strategies, including all of the ones I am sharing in this book, or you may just snap out of it on your own. But if a System Upgrade is indeed taking place, none of your go-to moves will work or have the same effect that they normally do. Or they might work for a moment or two, but then you find yourself feeling low again, unable to recover well or have your usual clarity. You may notice that you have forgotten or don't seem to have access to all of the truths you thought you knew about life. You just don't feel like yourself and it feels really, really uncomfortable and sometimes even scary.

It is during these times that it is particularly useful to stop and take a step back, take a big, deep breath, and remember the following:

- *You are now encountering a significant spiritual growth spurt.* A huge leap in your spiritual evolution is about to happen and what you are currently experiencing are simply signs of that.
- *There is no need to beat yourself up about what's showing up.* You did nothing wrong. It was actually going to happen no matter what and it is all very, very good. In fact, as you increase your awareness of this, you may begin to recognize what's happening sooner and may even celebrate these times, as weird as that sounds.

- *Surrender.* There is no need to try to "fix" anything. In other words, the misalignment you are feeling (which can be expressed as stress, anxiety, fear, worry, doubt, etc.) is best managed when you shift your focus *away from* the things that you are fretting over. Don't try to solve the problem in the same energy that it exists in; simply remind yourself of this and put these challenges on a shelf to be looked at again when you are back in alignment. Trying to figure things out from a place of misalignment will only create more resistance and keep you in this part of the process longer.

- *You are not alone.* Upon surrendering to and embracing what is happening, it is really helpful to say a prayer or mantra such as, "Thank you, God/Universe, for the gift in this experience, even if I don't understand it yet," or "Thank you, God/Universe, for helping me to remember that all is unfolding perfectly."

- *The discomfort is temporary.* You **will** get to the other side of this, and it will be so worth it.

- *Shift your attention to things that feel good, and recognize that what may feel good in this context might not be the same as what feels good to you when everything is peachy.* In this context, things that feel good may look like taking a nap, sobbing uncontrollably, screaming into a pillow, watching indulgent television, or eating ice cream. Go with it, reminding yourself once again that this is all temporary.

- *Give yourself permission to trust that all is unfolding perfectly and you are indeed taken care of by the Universe.* It's **TEMPORARY**.

- *Know that there are **huge** gifts on the other side of this, and when you do hit that "breakthrough" part, you will know it.*

The breakthrough part is a Godsend. It feels like relief, release, and a sense of well-being you haven't felt in seemingly forever. You feel lighter, clearer, have more energy, and feel like you're back to your old self again, except you are somehow different. You are indeed a newer, higher version of yourself. You may or may not be able to identify the specific changes that have taken place, but you will probably notice that life just seems better, perhaps even easier, and more joyful.

It took me a long time to get this. And when I finally began to get it, it took me a long time to apply it. But once I did, it became easier and easier. I was able to recognize what was happening sooner and get myself into a state of surrender and allowing, which took away the majority of the pain, though maybe not the discomfort. I even began to look forward to the new growth that I knew was coming each time I found myself in breakdown mode.

I remember one "growth spurt" in particular that happened a couple of years ago. To the naked eye, it looked something like this: I began skipping some of my daily practices that contribute to my state of alignment and well-being because I decided it was the weekend and I didn't have the time for it. My three-year-old was around me nonstop, and I was deeply fatigued from being in the early stages of pregnancy with my second child. So I went four days without meditating and barely gave it a second thought. Skipping my habits tends to be a huge sign for me, but I wasn't aware of this at that point.

My husband had also gone out of town for work and I found my hormonal, tired self absolutely dreading the next four days, anticipating them to be difficult without him home. It is unlike me to have such a dire perspective on things, or to not, at least, attempt to change that perspective.

My three-year-old pushed every button I had, and what had already been over a year of struggling with potty training seemed to come to a head during that time–she had seven accidents in one day.

Other signs included getting pulled over by a cop for speeding, receiving an email from a client requesting to put our coaching on hold due to financial issues (something a self-employed coach never likes to hear), finding out someone spent $780 with my credit card (making me a victim of identity theft for the first time), and the grand finale was my curtain rod falling down and hitting me on the head...twice.

It was right at about the fourth time my daughter had an accident, at a restaurant no less, that I began to realize what was happening. I wasn't quite ready to celebrate the growth spurt at that point, I'll admit, but it did give me that relief that all of this was happening for a higher purpose. It also gave me permission to not try to fix any of it, nor worry about it. I recognized that I was way out of alignment, and therefore my only job at this point was to follow what felt good, as best as I could manage. All of the above things would either work themselves out as a result, or at the very least I would be in a much better place to handle them. Shortly after putting all of this together and surrendering to it, the fog lifted and I was on the Breakthrough side, which I just knew because the relief is so palpable.

The Bottom Line

In short, you can direct the flow (though not necessarily the details) of your life 95% of the time through the conscious and consistent managing of your vibration, thoughts, and emotions by using the tools I've covered so far and many others I haven't. But when a Breakdown before the

Breakthrough or Spiritual Upgrade occurs, there's virtually nothing you can do but ride it out and allow it to happen. The more you resist it, the more difficult the experience will seem. Yet if you can acknowledge what's happening, trust in the process, and shift your focus to things that feel even a little bit better, you'll be through it in no time and reaping the benefits. Well, you'll reap the benefits no matter what, but you'll enjoy the satisfaction of knowing you navigated it consciously and intentionally, and therefore less painfully.

Breakdown before the Breakthroughs happen at different lengths of time, at different levels of intensity, and there doesn't appear to be any rhyme or reason as to how often they occur. Sometimes they happen and you may not even notice; they may not even be experienced as painful or challenging. In my experience, the bigger the Breakthrough, the more you will notice it. But no matter what it looks like, you will know when you are on the other side of it. You will feel a sort of lightness, a dissipation of that heavy, intense energy that was present before. Confusion turns to clarity and you will feel like your old self again, except somehow different. Oftentimes you will be able to identify what exactly is different, such as an old belief not having much power over you anymore or a burst of energy and clarity in a certain area of your life. Other times you may not be able to name it, yet you are aware that you feel different, and it's a good feeling.

I felt it hugely important to include this chapter in this particular book because I am certain everyone experiences this phenomenon and suffers because they don't realize that it's an actual phenomenon! Just knowing that you are not alone and not at fault when your world seems to be collapsing is such a relief, and knowing that there are ways you can flow through it is extremely valuable. But even though you will continue to have these upgrades throughout your life, I urge you not to waste any energy dreading them. They do get easier, and you will always be happy with the result.

Practical Application:

Below I have summarized the Breakdown before the Breakthrough phenomenon, and I encourage you to copy it on another piece of paper, perhaps even laminate it, and post it somewhere you can see it often to aide you in recognizing what's happening when these "System Upgrades" occur. Also, when one does happen, get out that journal and write about it. Process your feelings, don't try to push them away or force yourself into a state of positivity–just be with it instead. When it's complete, and you'll know it when that happens, make a note of what new things emerged from within you. In other words, what happened as a result of this spiritual growth spurt? Who are you now? What new understandings or desires do you have? What are you going to do with them?

The Breakdown before the Breakthrough...and What to Do!
What it is: It is essentially an upgrading of your energetic "system," when you are ready to become the next highest version of yourself. You are being "broken down" so that you can energetically be "put back together" as a *higher-functioning* you.

Identifying Characteristics: The biggest sign that you are experiencing one is that all of your other "go-to" moves for feeling good and getting aligned fail, or don't seem to work as well. It is also marked by feeling down, more than usual or for longer periods of time, an unusual number of bad or unwanted things seem to be happening, you consistently feel overwhelmed, and you seem to almost forget what you know about life. While the breakdown period can be very uncomfortable and intense, the Breakthrough period feels wonderful, and the shift is something you "just know" has happened. It feels like relief, clarity, certainty, or feeling like yourself again, yet somehow different. You may or may not be able to identify the specific aspects of your new self, but you will definitely feel different.

What you can do:

- Acknowledge what is happening and surrender to it. It's going to play out with or without your resistance, so by choosing to embrace what's happening you are allowing yourself to go through it with more ease and grace. This usually results in a shorter duration of the Breakdown phase.

- Pause and give yourself a moment to say, "Thank you, God/Universe, for the gift in this experience, even if I don't understand it yet," "Thank you, God/Universe, for helping me to understand that all is unfolding perfectly," or "I will let whatever happens be okay." Trust that every single thing that is unfolding is for your highest good, even if it doesn't look like it.

- Allow yourself to feel whatever you feel without judgment, and give yourself the space to take care of yourself. Remember that what feels good during this time might be different from what typically feels good to you. If it feels good to take the day off and watch TV all day, then do it. If it feels good to cry, or hide out from others, do it. Remember that this is temporary.

- When you feel the shift, and you will know it when it happens, celebrate and enjoy your new self!

CHAPTER 9
PERSPECTIVE IS EVERYTHING
AND ASSUMPTION IS THE DEVIL

"Quantum physics tells us that nothing that is observed is unaffected by the observer. That statement, from science, holds an enormous and powerful insight. It means that everyone sees a different truth, because everyone is creating what they see."

~ *Neale Donald Walsch*

Perspective 101
1. **Something happens.**
2. **It means nothing.**
3. **We make up a story about what it means.**
4. **The story we make up creates our reality, it creates our world, it creates what's possible and not possible.**

(From a Facebook meme-source unknown)

My mom and I share a joke where when one of us doesn't call or text the other back in a timely manner, the other gets all hurt and offended. When we finally get ahold of one another the response is usually something like,

"Are you mad at me?" or "Oh, being a little passive-aggressive now, are we?" followed by some chuckles. We laugh because this has been a long-standing topic between us, how easy it is to make assumptions when we don't have all of the information, and how we usually jump to the most negative versions.

My mom is the first to admit this about herself, and she has made leaps and bounds of progress with it. She, like a lot of us, had the bad habit of making assumptions when people didn't call or text her back right away. She would immediately assume that person was punishing her or being rude on purpose, and would even go so far as to make up a story about why that was, which wasn't at all based on any factual evidence. Whenever we spoke about it, I would gently give the suggestion that perhaps she is making an incorrect assumption, remind her how, more often than not, she comes to find out her assumption wasn't at all true, and that she even tends to feel silly for getting so worked up in the first place. She would then agree and move past it, yet do the very same thing all over again the next time it happened.

One day I asked her if she'd like to skip the whole "making up a story" part and go straight to the understanding. Being the Italian spitfire she is, she at first gave it a nonsensical "You are!" in retaliation (our go-to phrase when we don't want to admit or deal with something). But a lightbulb went off for her, and after that I kept my mouth shut as I watched her begin to notice her habit on her own. Nowadays, we joke about it, and she calls me out when she notices me doing the same damn thing; we are all guilty of it. And if you've ever followed a negative assumption, you have seen how it can quickly escalate and come back to bite you.

I say assumptions are the devil flippantly because they really can get you into trouble. As humans we are so good at making stories up when we don't have all of the information needed to see things clearly. Brené Brown says in her book, *Rising Strong*, "in the absence of data we will always make up stories. It is how we are wired." If you pause and look at the world around you, at your own experiences of interaction and that of your loved ones, you will notice this to be alarmingly true. Our tendency to make stuff up, and usually the worst-case scenario of it, is at the root of so many misunderstandings and grudges we hold or arguments we've engaged in. And it's simply because we do not have all of the information, nor do we ask the right questions to get said information.

Brown offers the following valuable questions to ask when we encounter this:

- What more do I need to learn and understand about the situation?
- What more do I need to learn and understand about the other people in this story?
- What more do I need to learn and understand about myself?

Rising Strong, page XX

When one is caught in the messy web of assumption, these questions can instantly change the experience that is about to unfold for the better. Pausing long enough to consider each allows us to interrupt our usual pattern of having a knee-jerk reaction that isn't necessarily based in truth, and allows us to consciously respond to the situation instead.

This is information that I believe could change the world overnight if everyone had access to and applied it. I am willing to lay money down right now that if you stopped in this moment to look for some current assumptions you are making about any aspect in your immediate experience, you will come up with a few (at least). I can come up with at least three of my own right now:

Situation 1: A potential client hasn't emailed me back in almost a week.

- Assumption: She has changed her mind about working together.

Situation 2: Our daycare provider was short in her responses to my texts this morning.

- Assumption: She must be irritated with me about something.

Situation 3: I haven't been to kickboxing in a week.

- Assumption: The team that I am helping to coach must resent me for it.

If I were to choose to pause long enough to consider that I am only looking at each of these situations from my own limited point of view and am missing important information, such as the experiences of the other people involved, I would see that there is no need, and it is in fact impossible, to draw any accurate conclusions at this point. Furthermore, I could simply choose to make up something that feels better in the moment, realizing that only I am responsible for my own experience.

Did you get that? I am saying that the actual truth doesn't even matter in the largest sense; the missing information isn't even important. Because whatever your mind says about what is happening will determine your experience of it, *so you might as well make up something that feels good to you before you get the missing information you need.* I know it sounds like you're just lying to yourself, but what is actually happening here is conscious creation. By choosing a thought or perspective that feels good, you are creating the state of being that you want, one that will allow you to move forward in a higher vibration.

So, I could make up that:

Situation 1: The potential client got distracted by life and just hasn't gotten to it yet. It happens.

Situation 2: Our daycare provider had tiny humans pulling at her to feed them breakfast and couldn't give me more than a short response at that time. This also happens.

Situation 3: The students in my kickboxing group are well taken care of by the other coaches and know that if I'm not there then there is a good reason why.

There, that feels better! Having done my conscious and intentional work around this, I can now go about my day with a clean energetic slate.

Trigger Happy

Another thing to consider on this topic of perspective and assumption is that each of us has many areas in our lives where we tend to make assumptions automatically, things that act as embedded triggers. We react to these triggers unconsciously and like clockwork. We all have our unique triggers that cause us to react, due to our individual backgrounds and experience, but there is also the global kind, or the triggers that are common for most of us.

A common example is driving in traffic. Let's be honest here, we have all, at one time or another (or many), unintentionally cut someone else off while driving, or have been in a hurry to get somewhere and perhaps drove a bit aggressively. Or, conversely, we have driven too slowly because we were distracted by a conversation or were somewhat lost and trying to read street signs closely. In those situations we have likely pissed off other drivers, and have given it a

"Sorry, my bad" and moved on, because we were clear that this isn't how we typically drive. Yet the moment someone does any of those things to us we curse at them, roll our eyes, or say "Why are there such crappy drivers everywhere?! Get it together!" We are unconsciously making the assumption that this is how they must drive all of the time. This negative assumption leads to a negative reaction which impacts what we do next (oftentimes involving a certain finger).

Or how about when someone is rude to you, be it a stranger or a friend, and you immediately take it personally and assume that they are just an a-hole all the time? Ever done that? Who knows, maybe they are, but in all reality they are likely having a bad moment due to something that happened that you simply have no way of knowing about. I bet if you paused long enough, you could think of a time where you were unintentionally rude to someone else because of something difficult that happened to you, too. We are all human, we all have good moments and bad, and we are all reactive on occasion–in fact I'd say we are most of the time–yet we are rarely tolerant of it in others.

Again, if we choose to pause long enough to consider what our individual and global triggers may be, we stand a chance at interrupting the pattern and experiencing these things in a far more desirable way. Can you imagine all of the energy you might free up if you identified, even a few of, the triggers that were causing you to unconsciously react negatively, based on a perspective you've always held or an assumption you've always made? Think of what you could do with all of that free space!

An Even Larger Truth
But let's get back to what I was beginning to describe a moment ago. This isn't even about others, it's not even

about understanding or giving wiggle room to anyone else. I mean it is, sure, but there's something even deeper to understand and use here. Remember, we are all conscious co-creators, and the only thing that we can *solely* create is our experience of any given thing. When we choose to make it a positive experience, we are choosing to be our highest, most resourceful selves. We are choosing to express and directly experience Who We Really Are, and are exercising our power as creative beings. *We are who we say we are, and life is what we say it is, so if we find a way to make something good, we will experience it as good and that will be true for us—no matter what it is to anyone else.* Do you get the enormity of this?

Let's say you chose a perspective on something that causes you to feel good about it. For example, you missed your friend's birthday party due to a prior obligation. Rather than assuming she was is angry with you because you haven't heard from her in a while, you choose to make up that her silence towards you simply means she's got other things on her plate to think about. Little do you know, however, your friend is indeed upset with you and is intentionally choosing to give you the silent treatment. This fact ceases to matter if you behave based on your positive assumption, because you will be in a better place to act in alignment with your highest self. You will therefore have a more positive experience of what happens next, and you are giving your friend the space and option to do the same. After all, it is up to your friend to express her displeasure, not you, so why waste any time at all making up something that feels bad to you?

What I am saying here is that your perspective, and therefore your experience, of something trumps what may actually be happening.

You can, of course, repair the situation with your friend later on when you finally do talk. And if it were a situation where you were in the wrong, you could even own up to it and go from there. But by managing your energy through consciously choosing a perspective in the moment that serves, before you have all the information you need, you are allowing yourself to do all of that from a much better place versus one that might look like being defensive or reactive. Conversely, your friend has no idea what's going on in your head anyway, so everybody wins!

I know this is a big concept, and I understand that it will probably invite some protest. It may bring up the concern that choosing to live this way is irresponsible. But I'm also sure you've noticed a trend in this material by now: alignment. If you choose to live your life from a place of alignment as often as possible and strive to make decisions from this place in all you do, you simply cannot live life irresponsibly. Anything that happens as a result of your aligned chosen perspective and behaviors is valuable to everyone else around you, and it invites them to do the same. Ultimately, there is no such thing as a "good" or "bad" thing happening in our lives. There are things that happen and there is our response to it. It is wholly possible to have an event we would normally call "bad" be a very good experience for someone else, even the big ones. Through a lot of very dedicated and focused perspective and emotional/vibrational work, I would even call the sudden death of my own dad, my best friend, a "good" experience.

I don't expect you to get there right away; in fact, I rarely get there right away and this is my flippin' life's work. I am simply inviting you to experience your life in a new way by being more aware of your chosen perspectives and assumptions. I am inviting you to recognize that it's a choice in the first place, and that you can consciously choose the ones that support Who You Really Are and where you say you want to go in this life. I am inviting you to accept your God-given power and to use it. The best way to do that is through practice, and accepting that it's a life-long practice at that.

Practical Application:

What are some of your current assumptions we can clean up right now? What are some common ones you have conditioned yourself to make and react from? Take a moment to name a few out loud, and use the questions from Brené Brown above to help you navigate it. Here they are again:

- What more do I need to learn and understand about the situation?
- What more do I need to learn and understand about the other people in this story?
- What more do I need to learn and understand about myself?

Finally, what can you make up about these situations that feels better, and matches Who You Really Are? If you like, use the format below:

Situation 1: _____

Assumption:_____

Positive meaning I am giving it:_____

*__Bonus:__ Get into the habit of not taking action until you are in a better-feeling place. You can do this by practicing temporarily setting aside things that you have a strong negative reaction to, especially when you notice you're looking at them from a place of already feeling tired, overwhelmed, or stressed. Come back to the situation when you are feeling better, as your perspective will likely be more accurate, and you will be better informed as to what to do with it.

An example of this might be when you make that grave mistake of checking your phone and reading an email right before bed, or immediately upon waking when you're tired or groggy (something I don't recommend in the first place, and am also guilty of). Whatever you read is being read through a fatigued filter and is not likely being received the way it would be if you were awake, alert, and feeling centered. If this does happen, consciously choose to put the phone down, or play Scramble with Friends on it like I do, and come back to that stupid email later.

CHAPTER 10
SELFISH IS THE NEW SELF-LOVE

"If we were standing in your physical shoes, that would be our dominant quest: Entertaining Yourself, pleasing Yourself, connecting with Yourself, being Yourself, enjoying Yourself, loving Yourself. Some say, 'Well, Abraham you teach selfishness.' And we say, yes we do, yes we do, yes we do, because unless you are selfish enough to reach for that connection, you don't have anything to give anyone, anyway. And when you are selfish enough to make that connection–you have an enormous gift that you give everywhere you are."

~ Abraham-Hicks

I believe that selfish is the new self-love. Those words fell out of my mouth recently when coaching a client, and we both gasped and said, "Yes!" She even said I should coin that phrase and make products with it, which I still may do, so hands off!

We had been talking about how, for her entire life, she had been taught that "selfish" is a bad word and that putting yourself first was a big no-no, a story to which we can all relate to some degree. I had been using the "oxygen mask" analogy of putting your own mask on first before helping others on an airplane, a common one used in the self-development community. I was attempting to show her how she needs to be selfish in order to be a force of good and service in this world, when it hit me like a ton of bricks that it actually goes much deeper than that.

In the past decade or so, the self-development community has done an excellent job of beginning to shift the paradigm from "always put others first no matter what, even at the expense of your own well-being" to "fill up your own tank first so that you have the energy to give to and serve others." It has been a breakthrough perspective for so many, including myself, and I still believe it to be very true.

And yet, it isn't just about taking care of yourself first so you can take care of others, it's about taking care of yourself first because you are an incredible, magnificent being and you deserve it! This is what we came here for! Not only is it incredibly satisfying to focus on yourself and your own alignment and well-being, it is the very thing that catalyzes being Who You Really Are in the first place. You simply cannot ignore yourself or put yourself last when attempting to be your true self.

Being Selfish is a Gift to Others, Too

I get that there are plenty of you out there who are uncomfortable with the words above; I used to be as well. If you're like me, it's probably because you're thinking, "Aren't you forgetting the whole do unto others, serve the world thing?" It's also likely because you've been conditioned to think and believe that giving to yourself and liking yourself, much less loving yourself, are not acceptable things and actually indicate that you are somehow doing something wrong; old programming is coming into play. Yet for some of you it may be something wholly different, it may be because you've been on this conscious, spiritual path for a while and you have learned that loving yourself and giving to yourself are indeed important, but that a life serving others is a life well-lived. You are not wrong.

I am not talking about taking a hard stance on this topic, that you should either put yourself first or put others first and there is no middle ground. *I am talking about integrating this concept in a way that **gives you permission** to feel good about engaging in the stuff that brings you pleasure as a human, indulging in the things that nourish you as a spiritual being, and understanding deeply how giving to yourself and giving to others work hand-in-hand.* When you give to yourself, you are essentially giving to others. And when you give to others, you feel so good about it and it is a statement to the Universe that it is yours to give in the first place, that you are essentially giving to yourself, too. Everyone wins.

But here's the subtlety that I do not want you to miss. When you are focusing on your own well-being and alignment, consciously and consistently engaging in things that raise your vibration and get you into a state of resourcefulness more frequently, *you will find that you naturally want to serve others, and you will actually do so effortlessly just by being you.* Even if you didn't want to take some sort of physical action towards helping others and simply focused on your own well-being, walking through life with kindness and happiness, you'd still be serving mankind greatly because your high vibration benefits everyone and everything around you—it contributes to the collective consciousness of the planet.

Furthermore, being self-centered—that is, centered around the Self—is actually a really great strategy for living, because when you are self-centered in a loving, honest, aligned way, you are allowing yourself to walk freely on this planet without the burden of second-guessing yourself. You no longer have to be shrouded in self-doubt, wondering if you got it right or not. In other words, if you are coming from a place of alignment with any thought, word, or action, you will never have anything to apologize for and you will never be "wrong." When you get good at putting your own well-being and alignment first, you begin to learn and accept that when you do so there is no way that your choices and actions cannot work out for the highest good of all around you.

You see, it would be impossible to account for or take responsibility for the reactions and experiences of others that you are involved with. Attempting to take this responsibility would only lead to more complications and would probably lead to burn-out or a general throwing your hands up in the air yelling "I give up!" Each of us is only responsible for how we choose to show up, what we are putting into the collective human experience. What everyone else chooses to do with that is their gift, their opportunity of being a conscious co-creator on this beautiful planet. Even if how you show up seems to be received in less than a positive light, consider that the other person's initial negative reaction has caused them to re-evaluate and further define who they are and who they want to be. In other words, if someone is pissed off at you, it has allowed them to access parts of themselves they hadn't or couldn't otherwise access.

Remember, life is always working for each and every one of us—no exceptions. If it is there in your world, it is there for a reason. It is a gift you sent yourself, and it is up to you to open it.

The Mechanics of Being Selfish

We are, by now, clear that you are the engine of your experience, and if you are not well-fueled and all of your parts are not kept up through maintenance, then you will eventually break down. You will be of no use to anyone, and your quality of life will drastically drop. That part is not new and I'm sure you get it, but what may have not been entirely clear up to this point is the vibrational mechanics of how your being in alignment and feeling good works to benefit all. Allow me to break it down for you.

Do you remember earlier when I said that one person who is in vibrational alignment with Who They Really Are is more powerful than a million people who are not? This is what I was talking about. When one person takes the consistent, dedicated time and energy to focus on their own well-being and alignment, their vibration is consistently raised to a level that not only gives them access to their highest, most resourceful self, but *automatically lifts the vibration of those around them whether they are aware of it or not*. It creates a ripple effect of high-vibrating energy. How cool is that?

Think about it for a moment. How do you feel when you are around a truly, genuinely happy and well-balanced person? I'm not talking about the annoying kind, the ones that are giving you some forced-positive-attitude versions of themselves. I'm talking about the people who don't even have to say a word for you to know they are happy, the ones you can't help but instantly like, and the ones you notice effortlessly bring out the best in you. Or, have you ever noticed your kids or spouse feeding off your own high energy and good mood? It is like that, except it goes much further than what we may physically be able to observe. Your high vibration contributes to your family, friends, community, city, state, region, country, and the world—our collective consciousness. You are quite literally doing your part to "heal the world" when you are being selfish in this highest sense of the word.

This is the part where I want to tell you I could be totally wrong about this. I, of course, can't necessarily prove it and am merely passing along to you in my own words what I have received and learned from others along the way. Yet even if I were wrong about the vibrational "unseen" part, wouldn't it still make logical sense? Wouldn't it still be a very good and useful thing to allow your own happiness, kindness, resourcefulness, strengths, and gifts to spread like wildfire to those around you?

Practical Application:

It's time to put your researcher's hat back on, kids! I challenge you to take an entire week off from putting others first, and put your own happiness, preferences, and well-being first instead. This is for the sake of research, of course; how else are you going to truly know if I'm full of crap or not? Experiment with this, and if a week is too much for you initially, then just start with a day. A week is recommended so you can really observe the ripple effect, but I believe you'll see enough of a difference that first day to want to keep going.

Remember, it is extremely important that every element of your week of "selfishness" be preceded by alignment. In fact, be selfish enough to make sure you carve out and dedicate time each and every day for engaging in the practices that support your alignment or anything that raises your vibration, so that it's easier for you to come from your Highest Self in all you do. Also, I want to note that sometimes being selfish does look like giving to another; if in any given moment the thing you want most is to help another out, then by all means do it. Selfish in this context simply means pausing long enough and often enough to hone in on what will serve you the most, and trusting that it will in turn serve everyone else, even if it doesn't initially look like it.

Some questions to ask yourself as you move about your week:

- What would I love to do right now?
- What do I prefer here?
- What works best for me?
- What do I need in order to feel good?
- Is this that important to me?

Be ready to say no if you are given an offer that you previously would have said yes to out of obligation, and be willing to cancel and rearrange your schedule if what you are seeing doesn't actually sound that great to you. It's just a week; your world will not end if you do this, I assure you. It may be useful to set an alarm on your phone to give you reminders throughout your day to keep you in this self-centered space, and to take notes in your journal about what you are noticing along the way, such as:

- How am I feeling as a result of being more self-centered?
- How is it impacting others around me?
- How is it impacting the flow of my life?
- What is it showing me about my life and myself?

And when the week is up ...

- Did this experiment serve me? If so, how? If not, how?
- Who am I now?
- What do I want now?
- What are my new understandings?

CHAPTER 11
BE YOUR OWN BFF

"Perhaps we should love ourselves so fiercely, that when others see us they know exactly how it should be done."
~ *Rudy Francisco*

As I said before, selfish is the new self-love. We took a deeper look at the selfish part of that equation, now let's dive deeper into the self-love part. Our ability to be selfish in the highest way I just spoke of is dependent on our ability, or at least willingness, to love ourselves. I think for most people this is a really tough one, and most don't even know where to start. Yet, the inability to love ourselves well is from which each and every problem stems–challenge, hurt, issue, misunderstanding, and even world tragedy.

We were never taught how. Think about it. Did your parents specifically teach you about self-love? And if you happened to be the lucky kid whose parents actually made it okay to love yourself, did they ever actually give you specific skills to do it? Most likely, the answer is no.

In fact, most people can attest to being conditioned to believe the opposite, that it is *not* okay to love yourself, and that even thinking about it is being conceited, arrogant, and selfish. The same, perhaps to an even larger degree, is true for our parents' generation. And their parents'…and their parents'… and on and on…

From this cycle has sprung a gigantic tendency to focus on flaws, and not only our own flaws, but the flaws of everyone else. We have been trained to see what's wrong first, and as you're becoming more aware of, this is not to our benefit.

Lack of, or low, self-love shows up in our lives in countless ways. There are the big ones, of course, such as addiction, depression, eating disorders, relationship dysfunction, sexual dysfunction, violence, and suicide. But there are more subtle ones as well, including excessive people-pleasing, keeping ourselves overly busy and distracted, taking care of others to the exclusion of ourselves, being inauthentic for the sake of fitting in, staying in a bad relationship or friendship, being a doormat for others, and many more that I haven't named. It is like we project our energy in every direction other than nurturing the needs of our innermost selves, and we suffer for it.

When I work with my clients, this topic always comes up after digging into the various issues or challenges they are bringing to the table. Problems in your relationship? They are rooted in lack of self-love and connection. Tendency to engage in numbing behavior such as emotional eating or watching too many reality shows and can't seem to control it? Also, lack of self-love and connection. Can't seem to find your life's purpose? Once again, lack of self-love and connection. It's not the only thing behind each of these issues, but can definitely be found at the root.

This is *always* the place to look, the place I direct my clients to, when the time is right, and it really makes my job quite easy. I don't have to sit with clients and analyze why a certain pattern appears in their life over and over again because the answer is always the same. That is why our coaching begins with having the client engage in a set of daily habits or practices designed to focus them inward. When they do so, they are simultaneously cultivating self-love and a deeper connection with themselves. They are practicing the ability to shift their focus away from the outer world and place it inside themselves instead, where it is most useful. They quickly learn to care about how they feel, and their own well-being. Then, when that self-love topic inevitably comes up, they are not only ready for it, they are already halfway ready to practice it. It's like a shortcut, and I am such a fan of shortcuts.

Learning to love yourself without abandon is the most powerful of shortcuts. It is the cure to all of our ills. Notice I said "without abandon." When we engage in behavior with a focus that pulls us further away from ourselves, we are, quite literally, abandoning ourselves. I have a hunch that we have become so adept at abandoning ourselves, not because we're afraid that we'll find we're really not worth anything, but that we'll find out how amazing we really are. And that will change everything.

Life as we know it will cease to be, and that can be an incredibly scary thing, despite the actual end result being very good. Yet what would happen if we stopped doing this, we stopped running away? What would happen to all of our issues, problems, challenges, habits, and old patterns of thought and belief if we were to proactively start shifting our attention to loving ourselves as consciously and as fully as we can, every single day?

My Journey to Being My Own BFF

My two biggest patterns of self-abandonment have been emotional eating/being overweight as well as using my *chameleon superpower* (we'll talk about superpowers later—yes, you have some, too!) to blend in, by taking on the characteristics, mannerisms, likes, and interests of those around me. The latter allowed me to easily ignore myself by keeping my focus on those around me, giving me the comfort and safety of fitting in; there's always some sort of payoff to such behavior. The overweight issue was twofold: it gave me an extra layer of "protection," so that I could keep others away from me to a certain degree, and emotional eating allowed me to check out and deal with the unpleasant emotions and experiences I was having by simply numbing them, giving me temporary relief.

I know that's a common one for people, especially in America. And although I wrote that matter-of-factly as if it was a no-brainer that I've always been aware of, it took me years of every form of self-development work I could get my hands on to come to these conclusions. Fortunately, it was done in a manner that promoted self-awareness, self-acceptance, and the beginnings of conscious self-love. It's pretty much why I became a coach in the first place, though I wasn't aware of it back then. I thought I was doing it because I had an innate ability and desire to help others, which was also true, but the person I was looking to help the most was me.

In fact, it was in my initial life coach training through The Coaches Training Institute (CTI) where this self-abandonment issue stepped into the spotlight for me. CTI's training requires you to apply every concept learned to yourself first. Next, we had to practice on each other. The genius of the program is that once we used the system on ourselves and a partner we would know what the hell we were talking about when working with our clients, because all healing begins with the self.

It was my third or fourth month of training, I believe, where they had us identify what it was we couldn't "be with" in life; that thing that causes such an adverse reaction in you, and that you typically project onto others in the form of judgment. For me, the things I couldn't "be with" were those people who insisted on always having all of the attention, the ones who had to always make it about them in a super irritating, eye roll inducing sort of way. It has driven me nuts my whole life, and, oddly enough, I always seemed to be surrounded by people like that. Some of them have even been my closest friends. It wasn't even that it annoyed me because attention was being drawn away from me; I rarely wanted to be in the spotlight and it certainly wasn't comfortable for me (remember, chameleons like to blend in). It was that their attention-seeking behavior seemed so obviously over-compensating and inauthentic, and people fell for it left and right! How disgusting!

Through CTI's process we were guided to sort of "peel back the layers" of this thing that drove us so crazy, and trace its origins back to something within ourselves. Without going into all of those layers, here is what I found: I got so incredibly irritated, angry, "judge-y" and often down-right upset with those who seized the spotlight all the time because I was so afraid to do that myself. I was afraid to let myself be seen and known. I valued blending in because it was a great way to not have to let others see the real me, and whenever I encountered someone who claimed all the attention, it was a strong reminder of the pain I unconsciously felt about hiding Who I Really Am.

This was a huge "ah-ha" moment for me, especially when our instructors made us wear a nametag with our core issue written on it to go to lunch, while also "being in the energy of it" (acting it out). I had to sit with my fellow classmates at a public restaurant, wearing a nametag that said "Self-Abandonment" for all to see, and I had to maintain awareness and act in ways that exuded it for the whole lunch hour.

Talk about awkward and uncomfortable! It was very effective. You can imagine how ready I was to rip that nametag off, both literally and metaphorically, after that.

Following that experience, I became aware of my self-abandonment behaviors and strived to do a better job of loving myself. With the help of my coaches, trusted friends, and a whole slew of self-help books and programs, I got really good at cultivating behaviors that supported self-love instead of self-abandonment. Some of these behaviors included setting healthy boundaries with others, paying attention to what I wanted instead of just going along with another's preference, identifying my strengths and abilities and honoring them, stepping out more and allowing myself to be seen bit by bit, and sharing my gifts in a louder way. It also included choosing love and compassion more often when encountering someone with attention-seeking behavior.

The emotional eating thing even got better, though I admit that is still a work in progress, and is an expression of many other things I am growing from (that's a nice way of putting it, eh?). But perhaps the biggest progress I've made in that department, in addition to decreasing my emotional eating and taking much better care of my physical self, is that I am more accepting and loving when it does happen, and choosing to be gentle with myself. I'm actually not in such a hurry to overcome that one, surprisingly. I feel good about my efforts, progress, and the gifts and learning I am always gaining from it. I know that sounds weird but, perhaps for the first time in my life, it is true.

It Takes a Little Practice

This is just a guess, but I believe the above is possible for me because of the conscious and focused practices of self-love that I do every single day, without exception. I actively look for and acknowledge things to like, love, appreciate, and enjoy about myself. I even share them with others (gasp!) at times, gently swallowing the fear that they will give me a look like "really?" and roll their eyes. I also practice being okay–good even–with actively receiving from others. When someone compliments me, I pause, take a deep breath, and say "thank you" while making eye contact. I make sure to write it down in my journal if it was an especially good one, allowing myself to sit in the energy of it for a bit. If someone gives me a gift or does something nice for me, I don't try to talk them out of it with such words as, "Oh, you shouldn't have." I instead thank them deeply and genuinely, and allow myself to really be with how good it feels to know that someone cares for me that much.

Another way I practice self-love is through actively looking for things to love and appreciate in others. I help my clients work on this as well. As often as they can consciously remember to, they work on pausing to allow themselves to really see the people in their lives. The more they do it, the easier it is to do. This includes the core people in their life and those they meet in passing.

For example, one client was traveling for work so I challenged her to strive to see the beauty in everyone she encountered. She told me about her meeting with a customer, who was a striking Muslim woman with a radiant smile and very kind eyes, and my client told her as much. She smiled even bigger, and was a bit embarrassed and surprised, but my client could tell she felt really good upon hearing that. It made my client feel really good, too, not only because she caused another joy but because she got to express and experience a wonderful part of Who She Really Is. She told me that in the past, she would have been kind and polite because she was raised to be, but she probably wouldn't have noticed those things about her customer, much less said them directly to her. It probably would have gone right through her brain as "meet with this person, get the job done" and move on, barely remembering the experience. This new way is much more satisfying and fulfilling.

Everything in life is so much easier, more enjoyable, and more satisfying when you begin working on being aware of loving yourself more. It provides you with a strong foundation to handle any challenge or hardship, too, and choosing a self-loving behavior in any moment of difficulty will instantly diffuse it and remind you of Who You Really Are. But you have to be willing to go there.

I recently admitted to myself that I am my own best friend, and that there is no one on this planet I trust more than me. That is not said with a tinge of arrogance or fear-based thinking, such as "you can't trust anyone in this world but yourself!" On the contrary, I am blessed with more individuals in my life than I can count who I have the pleasure of trusting implicitly. But somehow saying that about yourself is a whole new level of gratitude, fulfillment, and satisfaction, like I feel privileged to be me.

It's funny, I've had a quote on the signature line of my outgoing emails for years now from Johann Wolfgang von Goethe that says, "As soon as you trust yourself, you will know how to live." How appropriate. This doesn't mean I don't have my human moments where I forget this. I will always have my human moments, and there are still plenty of layers to peel back and things to "work" on. But I think it does mean this is becoming my dominant way of being, of living, and my external world reflects it more and more. You can have, be, and do this, too.

Practical Application:

Add a section in your journal where you take the time to acknowledge, appreciate, and "own" the things you love about yourself daily. I call this section "What I Love About Me", or WILAM, and I list as many as I can access in that moment, no matter how small or insignificant they seem. It can be things like "I love that I am left-handed," "I love my smile," or "I love how much I care about others." It can even be about weird or subtle things like "I love my innate smartass" or "I love that I'm a little high-maintenance at times." If the word "love" is difficult for you to begin with, try using words that are a little bit more accessible, such as "like," "enjoy," or "appreciate," and allow yourself to get there at your own pace.

Also, begin really looking at people, as in consciously looking for the best parts of them. What stands out about them? What's beautiful or admirable about them? An easy way to remember to do this is when you notice someone annoys you; let that be your trigger or reminder to actively find something to appreciate about them. Work it out by writing it down in your journal. It's okay if you don't do it with every person you encounter throughout your day; even if you remember to do it once a day, it will make a big difference.

To Summarize Embracing Your Humanity....

- "Overcoming" your humanity is not the goal, nor is it necessary for you to be functional as Who You Really Are. In fact, embracing and loving your human self is perhaps the most direct path to this, because it lowers your resistance and powerfully assists you into a state of allowing.

- Getting rid of your ego is also not the goal. Rather, the goal is to use it for the purpose in which it's intended: as a means to self-identify. Living from your ego is only a "bad" thing when that is all you are doing, and you are ignoring your spirit.

- Practice embracing every single thing that shows up in your world as being there to serve a higher purpose, even if you don't yet understand what that might be. This not only brings relief and cultivates trust and certainty in God, your Higher Self, and life in general, but also allows you to be in a more resourceful state of being able to handle whatever challenge is present.

- It is absolutely okay to think a negative thought or feel a negative emotion. In fact, if you resist or attempt to talk yourself out of negative thoughts and feelings, they will persist and multiply. They are there to serve a higher purpose, like all things in life, and it is good to acknowledge and process them. The trick is to not stay there. After you've acknowledged and processed the negative thought, leave it there and shift your attention to something that feels better.

- Change is constant in our world, and there is a natural ebb and flow in life. Occasionally, there is an ebb called the "Breakdown before the Breakthrough," which occurs when we are ready to shed who we used to be in order to become the next highest version of ourselves. The breakdown phase generally feels confusing and painful, but doesn't need to be. Understanding the energetic components of what's happening can make all the difference during these inevitable and highly transformative times.

- Perspective determines behavior, which determines your experience. If a perspective does not feel good, seek to change it so that your experience of any given thing changes for the better. Remember that if a perspective is not a good-feeling one, it may be because it is lacking additional information, in which case you are working from assumptions that may not be true.

- Focusing on your own well-being and alignment is the best gift you can give humanity, including those in your immediate life. Putting the needs of others before your own, from a place of feeling depleted and misaligned, is never doing the good you think it is. You also deserve your own attention because you are an incredible being of light and love!

- Cultivating self-love and developing a true friendship with yourself will wipe away a huge percentage of your perceived issues in life in and of itself.

- Be gentle with yourself. It will serve you to keep your focus on what you are doing right and well, instead of what you are doing wrong or aren't doing enough of.

PART 3:

EMBRACING YOUR SPIRITUALITY

This section is about the parts of you and the parts of life that are not necessarily seen or common knowledge, yet perhaps play the largest role in Who You Really Are. They are the aspects of life that most are not aware of, and if they are aware, they are hesitant to fully embrace them because it is so far from what we've been conditioned to believe as a society. These aspects of life are also resisted by most due to the faith required to adopt an attitude of "believing is seeing" versus the other way around. Yet the resistance to fully embracing our spirituality is perhaps the largest factor keeping us from experiencing the fullness of our being and the fullness of life. Put simply, when our spiritual selves are fully embraced, a life of harmony and magic unfolds.

The concepts and techniques on the following pages are the ones that I have found to be the most useful, effective, and supportive in living a life of alignment with Who We Really Are, when practiced consciously and consistently. I've used them in my own life for the past several years with conscious intention and support, and have guided my clients and anyone else who is willing and ready to do the same. Give yourself permission to embrace them fully, if even only temporarily, to determine whether or not this is the best approach for you. And if it's not, what does it tell you about what might be?

CHAPTER 12
THE HOW IS NOT UP TO US

"Live life as if everything is rigged in your favor."

~ Rumi

There's this great gift that we've been given as spiritual beings having a human experience that few people are consciously aware of, and it is one capable of transforming your experience of yourself and life forever. I don't know if it's officially considered to be one of those "Laws of the Universe," but it probably should be because it is such an important component to living and creating consciously. Just for funsies, let's call it "The Law of the How." *The Law of the How states that when there are things that we want in life, figuring out "the how," or the details, of it coming to fruition is simply not our job; it's the Universe's job.* A friend and colleague of mine says that such details are "none of our business," which I find to be a fantastic perspective.

So, what *is* our job then? Our job is to:

- *Know and be clear on what we want.* This can be done by intentional thinking and reflecting, or through the process of experiencing contrast, otherwise known as "what we don't want." Contrast inevitably shows us what we do want (as discussed in Chapter 7).

- *Do our best to manage our vibration, and stay in a state of allowing as much as possible.* This looks like focusing on good things as much as possible, and processing the negative stuff that shows up without staying in it too long, followed by consciously shifting back to the good stuff.
- *Take appropriate action when we are receiving "the how" from the Universe.* Whether it comes as an idea or thought that we receive out of nowhere, a serendipitous conversation with a friend or stranger that yields exactly what we need to hear, or a sudden burst of energy and motivation to work on something–we should act on it. Follow it. There are many ways the Universe delivers on "the how," and it is up to us to listen and then act accordingly.

In other words, our job is to feel good as often as possible so that we are at a high enough vibration to catch those prompts, signs, cues, and opportunities that the Universe begins delivering to us the moment we "ask." If we are bogged down in the details, trying to force a solution or something to happen from a place that feels heavy and hard, our vibration drops and it is like the door through which the Universe makes its deliveries closes. We don't have access to any of it in those moments.

Often when we go into "fix it" mode or try to push things along, it only causes us to go into a deeper state of resistance. We get panicked, frustrated, anxious, stressed out, and the sense of urgency in creating something or solving the problem makes us work even harder. When this happens, we vibrate at a lower frequency, which makes it difficult for the Universe to deliver on its side of the deal. It's a vicious cycle! If this sounds familiar to you, don't despair.

Rest in the knowledge that a) we were all pretty much conditioned to think this way, so you're not alone, and b) it just takes a simple shift in your approach and practice to make all the difference.

If you want to look at it in more scientific terms, let's view it from a neurological perspective. As you may recall from our earlier discussion, when the brain is under stress it doesn't function the way we need it to. It is flooded with stress hormones and neurochemicals that limit our access to the resources (thoughts, ideas, inspirations, data, energy, drive, focus, etc.) that we need to move forward on any given task. For example, imagine losing your car keys. Here's what that might look like: you're running late, feeling stressed and anxious about the story you are making up about what will happen if you are late, and your brain begins to release those chemicals I just mentioned. You are scrambling around your house, checking every nook and cranny and perhaps cursing out loud, becoming more and more frustrated. You finally pause for a second to take a few deep breaths and collect yourself. You begin to feel a little bit better. You then turn around, look down at your hands and see they were there the whole time.

In this example, when you take a moment to relax and send some oxygen to your brain, you allow yourself to "see" more; you give yourself access to information that was limited a minute earlier. Your brain begins to function at a higher capacity when you allow yourself to relax. Put into energetic terms, the moment you slow down and relax, you step aside and allow the Universe to make its delivery.

I love this law because it is incredibly useful and functional when understood, and it is approachable to everyone because it can be explained in both spiritual and scientific or logical terms. When I am doing a training or speaking event that is not in a typical spiritual development setting, such as an employee training in a school or an office where the aim is to help the staff become more mindful, intentional, happy, and therefore more effective in their jobs, I deliver this purely in terms of neurology. And they love it! I enjoy it as well because I get to sound like I know way more about the brain than I actually do. (For the record, I am far from an expert in neuroscience. I took a couple of courses and trainings specific to coaching, which gave me a basic knowledge of how the brain functions in common human, life contexts.) They all learn to slow down and feel good more often, knowing that they are flooding their brains with good-feeling neurochemicals such as serotonin, dopamine, and oxytocin (impressed?) which allows them to be more resourceful and effective at their jobs and in their lives. Plus they become happier people—it's a double win!

The part I don't go into in these particular trainings, is the part about how when you are consistent with this feeling-good-more-often-and-allowing-the-Universe-to-take-care-of-the-how approach, you open yourself up to receiving those things you've declared at some point that you'd like to manifest. The Universe never says no to our requests; the form and the timing may be different from what we thought we wanted, but it never denies us. It is really a matter of whether or not we are in receiving mode; whether or not we are keeping that door open through our vibration.

A Little Experiment with the 'Ole Universe

Being that I've never been a fan of hard work, or at least not the kind that doesn't feel good or satisfying, I was super on board with this concept when I first came across it. It was like I could hear my soul saying, "Seeeeeeeeee?? I TOLD you so." (She can really be immature sometimes.) In fact, I distinctly remember a time where I had been receiving a lot of signs and prompts pointing me to the fact that I didn't have to work very hard in order to be a successful coach, which at the time meant my having a steady client load and income. It was on my radar because it was early summer and I was feeling that all-too-familiar urge to play hooky and do nothing but kick my feet up and enjoy the sunshine. Marketing, promotion, networking, and following client leads sounded awful to me.

I was also given a copy of an Abraham-Hicks book on this very topic, *The Art of Allowing*, which was one of my initial signs to relax more. After noticing the fourth or fifth sign, which was an actual, literal sign that said "Relax. Go Play," I decided to do a little experiment. I used the last two weeks of June to only do things I felt joy and pleasure in doing, work-related or not; I wanted to put this theory that you can relax your way *into anything you want* to the test.

This was not as easy as one might think, especially for the first few days. First, I was on a solo mission that was mostly in my head, so there was little to no objectivity and a good chance that I was just procrastinating or making this all up. Or worse, I was crazy. Second, it was really the first time that I had ever intentionally and consistently planned my days solely around what would be enjoyable, and devoid of "have-to's." Boy, was my ego and old programming trying to take the reins and talk me out of it, and it almost won a couple of times. But I decided this may be the only opportunity I would have to do it, so I moved forward with gusto.

I didn't do one ounce of actual "work" during those two weeks, aside from a few client sessions. In fact, I even rescheduled one because I just simply wasn't in the mood (I probably shouldn't admit that) and it didn't feel pleasurable to me. I filled my days with going to the pool, reading books out in the sunshine, going for walks with friends or meeting for lunch or coffee, taking naps, getting a pedicure, and even getting my husband to play hooky with me once or twice. It was amazing, and I just felt so *good*!

The results of my little experiment? During and after the two weeks devoted to relaxing and having fun, three people contacted me out of the blue wanting a complimentary session, two of whom became on-going clients. I landed two speaking gigs from sources that reached out to me, and was asked to be a guest on a podcast. All of this just fell into my lap without me lifting a finger or doing anything tangible to force them along.

This was the way I had always wanted to, and deep down believed I could, do business! Feel good, be happy, let your light shine, and allow your people to find *you*–I had my proof! To put it into perspective, back then I would go months without having any real prospects, and all the networking in the world didn't seem to yield any direct results for me; plus, I hated it. Here, I did nothing but enjoy the heck out myself for a focused, prolonged period of time, and, like magic, things that matched the description of what I wanted *just showed up*. This is something I would now describe as me successfully keeping the door to the Universe open. Oh, and that client I canceled on ended up thanking me, as it worked out better for her to reschedule, too.

The Universe's Invitation to Us All

So am I saying that all you have to do to get everything you want in life is have fun, relax, and feel good as much as possible? YES. That is exactly what I am saying, and unashamedly at that. That initial experiment, years ago, was just the beginning. I have repeated the process over and over again myself, and have taught my clients to do the same, holding their hands along the way as their minds tried to talk them out of it. I know how it sounds; it sounds too good to be true and it probably sounds really, really lazy. Yet, I stand by it. I can say with utter certainty and conviction that if all you ever did was find ways to honestly feel good and keep that vibration up consistently, you would find yourself encountering amazing versions of the things you have called forth, daily, including the energy and motivation to follow through on important tasks.

However, I will say that allowing the Universe to take care of "the how" is not an easy thing to always implement, and it requires a ton of practice, reminders, patience, and faith. I will also say that keeping the door to the Universe open doesn't always look like spending two weeks at the beach and not doing one damned concrete thing in the way of work. That was just my way, the way I preferred, and to this day the way I feel the most joy. I don't like to work hard; I like doing a whole lot of nothin', actually. But everyone is different, and at times it may look like actual concrete "work," yet the difference is in the vibration. It doesn't *feel* like work.

To use my example of client attraction, those two weeks could have just as easily looked like me doing a little bit of relaxing, followed by a burning desire to implement an entire marketing plan with enthusiasm, creativity, and joy. That would be the particular form of "the how" that the Universe was delivering to me. I'll say it again–the difference is in the vibration. It's not what you are doing that matters, it's the vibration behind it, or who you are *being* while you are *doing* it. There's a reason why I never seemed to have any luck when it came to following the tried and true strategies of running a business and gaining clientele; I didn't enjoy it and it caused me to feel bad, which in turn caused my vibration to be too low to receive what I wanted.

Therefore, it's very important to be clear on what feels good to you in any context of life: work, parenting, relationships, health, money, social life, spirituality, etc. It's important to know how you as a unique vibrational being operate, which we will look at more deeply when we talk about your "energetic blueprint." It is also very important that you don't compare yourself with others as you identify these things, because what works for some does not work for all. We all have different thoughts, ideas, strengths, and "weaknesses" that contribute to the vibration we hold about any given thing. When you know and EMBRACE these things about yourself, they are easier to pay attention to and act on, which then allows you to stay in the "flow" more often. For example, a coaching colleague of mine had great luck gaining clients through placing flyers on car windows, an idea that horrified me. Her vibration around it was different than mine, so it was easier for her to receive "success" from it. Had I gone out and done the same thing I am sure I wouldn't have had such luck.

There is another important aspect of this law that I want to highlight: Practicing allowing the Universe to take care of "the how" simultaneously builds, strengthens, and expands your relationship with your Self, with God, and with the world around you. It creates a level of trust and certainty that I believe we are all desperately seeking and craving, and when nurtured and cultivated has the potential to help us live this life on a whole new level beyond our current imagining, including my own. Being in tune and in sync with the Universe is a huge reminder of Who We Really Are and the magic that we hold.

I would say by now I am fairly practiced at implementing this law, yet I have only scratched the surface of what is possible with that kind of connection and trust. It cultivates the feeling and experience of being a part of something bigger than yourself, of there being grander things than our eyes can see, and with that comes hope, gratitude, love, joy, and peace. Imagine if we all felt these things more often. Imagine what the collective vibration of this world would be. Wars would end, hunger would cease, and conflict would diminish. Keep this in mind as you are practicing this law. Your happiness and partnership with All That Is is the greatest gift you can give humanity. Is that enough to get you to follow through?

Practical Application

Copy the following and post it where you can see it as a daily reminder:

My Job:
- **Know what I want, at least the essence of it.**
- **Feel good as often as possible so that I can keep the door open for the Universe to deliver it in the form I asked for or one better that I haven't thought of yet.**
- **Know what feels good to me.**
- **Follow the prompts, cues, thoughts, and inspirations as they show up, and take inspired action.**

The Universe's Job:
- **Take care of all of the details of my requests and desires, including the form, timing, people, places, situations, ideas, thoughts, inspirations, energy, and any other components included in the delivery.**

Make it your highest priority to do your job, especially the feeling good part as often as possible. When stressed, find a way to relax. When overwhelmed, take a break and go do something fun. In fact, don't even wait until you are stressed or overwhelmed; be proactive with this and include fun, pleasure, play, and relaxation every single day without fail. Watch how your vibration rises and opens you up to more possibilities, options, and even miracles.

CHAPTER 13
ALL WORK AND NO PLAY
MAKE JACK A DULL BOY

"Hard work is not the path to Well-Being. Feeling good is the path to Well-Being. You don't create through action; you create through vibration. And then, your vibration calls action from you."

~ *Abraham-Hicks*

Do you want to know a secret? Sometimes I get so tired of all of this self-development, spiritual development, conscious awareness, and live-life-the-right-way stuff. Sometimes I don't want to think about any of it, don't want to worry if I'm doing it right, giving it my best, or working hard enough. I just want to go play, be light, and laugh a lot.

Then I remember that play, pleasure, and fun are actually very spiritual and hugely important in our own personal and global evolution; there's a reason why people are always "working for the weekend." I believe that each of us, no matter what walk of life or belief system we come from, knows intrinsically the value of kicking up your heels, relaxing, and goofing around. I believe somewhere deep down we all recognize it is our true nature, and is actually one of the best ways to get anything done.

Yet I also believe we have this work-hard-play-hard paradigm backwards, especially in the U.S. We have it hammered into us at an early age that working hard is the only way to get what you want, that relaxation and pleasure come only after they are earned, and "play" is typically a word used only in reference to children. We are taught there is honor and pride in hard work, which there is, of course, but productivity and busyness are glorified and almost worshipped and taken to an extreme. This misperception in priority leads to imbalance in our lives.

This imbalance gets expressed in several unpleasant ways, such as stress, illness, moodiness, depression, fatigue, and burnout, among others. Don't get me wrong, there is absolutely value in working hard; no one can deny how good the feeling of accomplishment is when you've poured your blood, sweat, and tears into something that is important to you. There is nothing wrong with the pride you feel in the finished product, not to mention what you learn about yourself along the way. But there is also the enormous amount of stress, pressure, overwhelm, sacrifice, and even illness that can come with this approach that seems to get ignored all too often. I think it's really important to shed some light on the fact that, contrary to popular belief and perception, all of the above is not a necessary component to achievement and productivity.

Furthermore, when considering the role of the *Law of the How* in our daily lives, as discussed in the previous chapter, working hard before allowing ourselves any kind of fun or downtime makes this law incredibly challenging to work to our advantage. How can we allow the Universe to work its magic for us if we are in a constant state of stress and overwhelm, continually trying to force things along?

Flipping the Paradigm

The approach I would like to offer here is the exact opposite of what we've been taught, and although it is the road less traveled, I have found it to be deeply, deeply effective and enjoyable in my own experience. Put simply: *play, pleasure, fun, and relaxation are not to be put off until the hard work is done, but are the very things that lead to productivity in the most satisfying and fulfilling sense.* This is because they a) allow your brain to relax, which puts it at an optimal state of functioning, and b) raise your vibration high enough to get you to a state of allowing, where you are more able to access ideas, energy, inspiration, motivation, and answers. The result is enjoying your work, and producing more!

In other words, allowing yourself to *feel good first* naturally and effortlessly leads you to the very things you need in order to be effective and productive, or be the person you need to be to get the job done. Doesn't that sound so much better than the simple plow-forward-and-work-hard-at-all-costs approach?

As a business owner and entrepreneur whose success relies solely on myself, I often get asked what I do to keep the flow of clients and income going, and usually those questions are specific to which particular marketing approaches I use. People are always surprised to hear that I use little to no marketing at all. I had one client actually make fun of my website, and I laughed right along with her because I was clear that it wasn't my website getting clients through the door, nor was it any other marketing efforts.

As I discussed before, it was my vibration, my willingness to put the majority of my energy towards feeling good, which did not include any of the traditional business strategies. I was much more interested in things that allowed me to play and have fun, relax and feel good; I could regale you with stories about how I have landed a client just by going to get my hair done at a swanky salon, or having chosen to take a nap instead of writing a newsletter to market my programs, and then later opening up an email from an ideal prospective client that seemed to find me out of the blue.

These weren't just random occurrences or things that happened every once in a while; this is how I have run my coaching business for the past five years. And I've been very successful. The marketing and promotional stuff that I have done when running a workshop or a group program was also done after I got myself into a good-feeling, resourceful state, which usually looked like having lunch with a friend, going to kickboxing, or spending time outside in the sun. I can also attest that the classes, workshops, and programs that I have for one reason or another created from my previous "work-hard-play-hard" mindset, didn't do as well. *Thus, I have learned to line up my energy to do what I need to do by playing first, so that I can work hard without it feeling like work.* I teach my clients the same strategy, and they all report happier, more fulfilling lives.

Yet, I understand that there are plenty of you out there who would just not align with the specifics of my approach because it doesn't match who you are, or it's just too big a leap to make from where you sit. So let me be clear that the manner in which I choose to engage in play, fun, and pleasure is specific to me, and yours might look vastly different. It may even look like something that falls under the category of "work," but that you, yourself, take great pleasure in.

For example, I have a friend who teaches yoga, and her form of pleasure for getting into a highly resourceful state of being is, well, yoga. That works for her. I also have a client who wishes she could spend hours creating charts and graphs that represent the various areas of her life, because she loves that sort of thing. She uses that form of pleasure to line up her energy for important tasks and projects, whereas I might just go to a movie. Again, it works for her.

Your challenge is to determine what works for YOU, and you will know what that is based on how good it feels to you, not whether anyone else does it that way or even if it makes logical sense. The essence of it is all the same: feel good first and then watch yourself "work hard" while enjoying yourself, and without all of the stress, overwhelm, and pressure that you used to feel.

Hitting the Reset Button

When applying this approach, it is also important to remember that you will likely need to hit several "reset buttons" throughout your day. What I mean is, even when we are consistently engaging in things that feel good to us and finding that we are working more efficiently and joyously as a result, we cannot be "on" all the time. It is natural to pop in and out of alignment throughout the day, and rather than giving up and succumbing to old ways of thinking and being, you can just simply start over again.

I refer to this as a "rinse and repeat" mindset. When something happens that knocks us out of alignment, whether it's hearing bad news, having an unpleasant interaction with someone, or simply feeling tired, we just need to hit the reset button and recalibrate our energy. In human terms, this looks like taking a break and doing something fun or relaxing to get yourself back in the flow again, even if that means allowing yourself to be done for the day. This, of course, requires a high level of self-awareness and paying attention to your feelings so that you can properly navigate it. But with practice, it's very doable and extremely rewarding.

Let's put all of this heady concept stuff into a real-life scenario to help integrate and reinforce your understanding. A client of mine wanted help with the launching of her coaching and consulting business. As she was working on the many aspects of the launch, such as building her website, creating her logo, and writing content that was useful for her target audience, she became overwhelmed with all of the emotions that came up, saying that at times she was sure she was bipolar. In one instant she felt like she was an absolute genius, and in the next she was sure she had no business attempting such a feat. Thoughts of "I'm not good enough," "What will people think?" and "Will I ever get this done?" popped in all too often and made it difficult for her to complete her tasks.

Creating anything from scratch, especially if it's really important to you, can be a really vulnerable experience. Furthermore, if it's coming solely from you, the process can be deeply isolating. There are moments when you've got no one or nothing else but your own thoughts to turn to. When my client asked for my help with the launch, she wasn't talking about the concrete components of how to create and launch a brand—I'm probably the last person you should ask about that. Instead, she wanted to know how to manage her energy and emotions so that she could get the job done well and enjoy doing it. So I guided her through the very method I am sharing with you in this chapter.

Each day I had her line up her energy to get herself into a peak emotional state, or a state of allowing, so that she could allow the material to come through her versus trying to force them out from just her brain. She had already identified that the latter didn't feel good to her, and she was clear that the services she was offering were also not coming solely from her brain. When she found herself hitting that place of trying to force inspiration to come through, which happened almost every day, I instructed her to back off and go relax or play. For her, this looked like taking a nap or a shower, sitting outside in the sun reading a book, meeting up with a friend, or going to a movie by herself, something she loved to do. Then she would simply come back to working, but from a higher energetic space. If she couldn't manage to do that in the same day, she would allow herself to rest, relax, and take pleasure in whatever ways she could for the rest of the day, knowing and trusting that it would contribute to the flow the next morning.

In our next session, two weeks after creating this plan together, she reported being much more productive and at ease with the whole process. She noticed it felt less and less like work, and would even wake up eager to get started. She had her "ducks in a row" for the launch in less time than she had anticipated, and the launch itself was successful. She later told me that if she had continued to attempt the "old school" way of plowing through until it got done, she would have probably given up completely. In fact, she follows this approach to this day and even teaches it to her own clients.

This doesn't just apply for people who are in a position of working for themselves, by the way, though it is admittedly a bit more challenging to apply when you are working for someone else. You may not be able to walk away from your desk and go to a movie in the middle of the workday, but you can certainly remove yourself for a moment to go outside for a brief breath of fresh air, or hide in the bathroom to meditate for a minute or two. This is where it gets perhaps even more useful to work with someone personally on these techniques and concepts, so that you can identify ways that fit your environment and life "framework" more closely. However, even if you just make sure to include play, pleasure, fun, rest, and relaxation in each and every day, it will make a big difference.

I know I've been using traditional career/job type stuff when referring to the term "work," but I intend that word to mean anything that feels like it: cleaning the house, getting ready for an event or party you're hosting, dealing with the challenges of relationships, parenting, daily interactions with others, reaching a goal of some sort–any context where it feels more like "work" to you, or feels hard. My husband and I have friends that designate Sundays for cleaning and house projects, which seems to do the trick for them so no judgment there, but to my husband and I that just sounds awful. Our weekends are golden, and we will soak up and take in every single ounce of play, fun, and relaxation there is to be had and leave the housework type stuff for later. I'm not sure if he thinks of it this way or not, but I know the dusting and vacuuming will be much easier and will probably go more quickly if we are doing it in a rested, relaxed state.

Thus far, you may have noticed I have been heavily emphasizing the concept of meeting yourself where you're at, and I'll do so again here. Meeting yourself where you're at in terms of play, fun, pleasure, and relaxation means embracing your inner nature and working with it rather than against it. The reason our work or the things that we want to accomplish in life feels so hard is because the way we are going about it is not natural to our spirit or to our essence, and our soul is indicating this through our feelings. So meet yourself where you're at and start allowing in and prioritizing more of the good stuff that you are made of! Make it your "work" to play, have fun, and be joyful first, and watch things come together much more smoothly and with greater satisfaction. But don't take my word for it; try it yourself through the exercise below.

Practical Application

Start a running list of all of things that you find to be plea-surable, enjoyable, playful, fun, and relaxing. If it helps, ask yourself what you'd be doing with your time if you had all of the time and money in the world and didn't even have to work, as this really helps you get to the heart of it. Once you have a good number of items on your list, make it a priority to do AT LEAST one thing from it each day. Schedule it in to your calendar so that in-the-moment life stuff doesn't tempt you to put it on the back burner. Adopt the perspec-tive that it is *a part of your work*. And if you're a real go-getter who is more than ready to put this concept into practice, fill your day with these things. Use them to "line up your energy," as described above, prior to engaging in the things you might call "work." Finally, keep adding to this list. It is so good for your soul, as they say, but it is also so good for your physical, human self.

Number a page in your journal from 1–10, 50 or 100 and title the page:

Things I Love To Do For Play, Fun, Pleasure, And Relaxation.

Now, fill it in and keep adding to it to your heart's content.

CHAPTER 14

YOUR ENERGETIC BLUEPRINT—
AND DID YOU KNOW YOU
HAVE SUPERPOWERS?

"The more in vibrational sync you are with who you really are, then the more you are allowing only those things that you're wanting, and the less resistance there is. And the less resistance there is, then the less delay between the idea of the thought and the receiving of it."

~ Abraham-Hicks

Okay, so head's up, the following concept is my own creation and is still evolving. If it feels like a bit of a stretch to you, that is good. I am trying to bring you out of your comfort zone. In fact, one day I will probably write an entire book about it, but am only going to do a brief overview to help you get started here. I have found it to be one of my most valuable self-discoveries. It is at the top of the favorite list for my clients as well because they find it to be so useful for living their spirituality in a functional way.

What is your Energetic Blueprint? In short, it is *the vibrational way in which you intrinsically function as the unique human and spiritual being that you are, determined by your soul prior to entering this lifetime.*

I am speaking about the *underlying energy behind* the differences in general human diversity. I mean, in addition to our genetics and environment, the reason we all have different personalities, traits, learning styles, preferences, strengths, etc., is we have all entered this lifetime with a specific and intentional energetic makeup. There are things that we naturally flow or vibrate with and things that we naturally don't, based on our soul's agenda for this life. Think of it as energetic DNA, and instead of focusing it on the physical things that we inherited from the combination of our parents' DNA, the energy focuses more on the aspects our souls chose to include in the makeup of our physical form. The point of all of this is to allow us *to be who we came here to be.*

When we are unaware of these very natural energetic components of our being, and are striving to instead fit into the "normal" confines of our culture and society, it can create a huge disconnect from our innermost self. There's an internal "rub" there that is difficult to name but is easily felt. Conversely, when one is aware and accepting of how their energy naturally flows, and consciously works with it, one can create great harmony within oneself and in life. If this is hurting your head so far, allow me to give you a hypothetical scenario to illustrate this.

Amy thrives on being busy. She is constantly juggling more balls than the average person should be able to happily handle, and her friend, Janet, can't help but feel intimidated by all that Amy effectively manages. So Janet attempts to emulate Amy's approach, convincing herself that she, too, can be Wonder Woman and handle it all at once. But in no time at all, Janet becomes overwhelmed and resentful of all she has on her plate. She even begins to judge Amy for her choices, adamant that there's no way she can truly be happy living like that. She shakes her head in contempt with each new project, event, or activity she hears her friend is involved in.

Janet then begins to judge herself, feeling bad that she can't seem to handle having her kids in a sport or activity six days a week and serve on the PTA, while also taking her Zumba and Spinning classes, finding time to organize fundraising events, *and* have dinner on the table every night. As a result, Janet becomes less resourceful and present in her life, stuck in self-loathing and judgment; she is convinced she's doing it wrong.

Janet continues on this path until one day she is having a conversation with another friend who is talking about this fantastic new book she's reading that explores the idea that we all have our own unique "Energetic Blueprint." The book describes that it is vital to our well-being and happiness to identify what some of the components of our Blueprint are, and strive to honor them in our daily choices. Janet, feeling a spark somewhere deep inside her, asks for the title of the book and name of this no doubt incredible author, thanks her friend profusely, and runs off to get a copy.

A week later she is basking in the peace, joy, satisfaction, and clarity she has knowing that she just isn't built the way Amy is built. That while Amy is naturally drawn to and thrives with variety, a fast pace, being around others, and lots of movement–all part of her Energetic Blueprint– Janet happens to be drawn to and thrives with having plenty of down time, being slow and intentional, having time at home with her kids doing nothing, and enjoying a good amount of solitude to reflect and take it all in. Both Amy and Janet feel at their best when they honor these natural inclinations. Neither of them is wrong, nor better than the other, they are just made up of different stuff. If Amy were to all of the sudden decide that she needed to be more like Janet, she would also quickly find herself in a very dissatisfied, perhaps self-loathing and judgmental state.

Here's the part I don't want you to miss: I'm not talking about personality traits, I'm not even talking about individual values. **I am talking about the deepest core essence of each individual** *creating their personalities and informing them of their values.* Your soul chose to love classical music, while your spouse's soul chose to love hardcore rap, ahead of time. And when each of you listens to your preferred music, you feel great.

And there's even more to it than that. Identifying and following your Energetic Blueprint, or natural flow of energy, helps you identify your path of least resistance in any given moment. That is, the path that will take you to your desired outcome more quickly, more easily, and with greater satisfaction than any other.

For Janet, who like any other normal human being desires a life of fulfillment, joy, and happiness, her path of least resistance is going to be one that encompasses the core components of her Energetic Blueprint that I named above. Anything that doesn't look like or feel like those components is going to feel extra challenging and heavy for her, and will ultimately not support or bring about the results that she's seeking. By working with her Blueprint, Janet is also saving herself a tremendous amount of wasted time and energy, by not making herself "wrong" (or judging herself) for focusing on things that she simply isn't an energetic match to. This is Janet's, and your own, "shortcut" to happiness around whichever context of your life you are looking at in any given moment, as well as a more direct path to merging with Who You Really Are. Isn't that great news?

Our Energy Changes Day to Day, and Over Time

I've been playing around with this concept long enough to notice that I am able to read or sense the natural flow of energy, or the path of least resistance, of each day and often even each moment. For example, when I wake up in the morning I seem to know within minutes whether it's going to be a social day or a quiet, introspective day. Or I know if it's going to be a kickboxing at the gym day or a workout at home day. I've noticed this isn't necessarily determined by my mood, either. I'm human and I have days where I wake up on the "wrong side of the bed," yet I can sense that the energy is flowing in a way that invites me to shift my mood up rather than indulge in it, so I am encouraged to do the necessary emotional and thought management work to get myself there.

I've also noticed that there are two kinds of resistance that show up for me: the useful kind that informs me that another direction may be of more benefit, and the illusory kind that is just wanting me to hide out and stay small and safe. The former type of resistance is based in intuition, and tuning into the present energy. The latter type is largely based in ego and false "data" from the mind.

Typically, if I even suspect that it's the illusory type of resistance I am feeling, I will push my way through whatever the task at hand is and come out on the other side feeling better for it. Just this morning, for example, I suspected this was happening when my brain was trying to tell me it was okay to stay home from kickboxing three days in a row and my body conspired along as it told me in no-uncertain terms that it didn't want to jump into my workout clothes, either. But I went and it felt great, and now I get to enjoy the freedom of not having to wrestle with my mind about fitting in a home workout or attempting to make peace with not working out at all. If you've been there yourself, then you know how mentally exhausting that can be.

Conversely, there have been days where I know with certainty that it is most beneficial to stay home. Most of the time I am not even clear about why, and oftentimes it doesn't even appear to make logical sense. To continue with the kickboxing example, at the beginning of each week I usually take the time to plan ahead which days I will go to class, but sometimes the energy of that day doesn't appear to match that intention. My logical mind says, "You have to go today, because you didn't go yesterday and you have another commitment tomorrow, so you better get your butt in there while you can." Yet, *vibrationally*, I just know and *can feel* that it's not where the energy seems to be flowing that day, whether it makes sense or not. Sometimes my brain will win and I will force myself to go, but I do notice those are the days I wish I hadn't. I end up feeling wiped out, instead of energized, for the rest of the day, I get a small injury, or I encounter crabby people while I'm out and about. I always come home thinking, "Okay, I get it, next time I will listen better."

When you get practiced in this concept, however, it is important to understand that just because the energy seems to be flowing in a specific direction does not mean that you absolutely have to follow it if you're to have a good day. It is simply a guidepost, I believe, illuminating the path of least resistance. We are all capable and have the inner resources to make any choice a good choice, or even the "right" choice. This is just a way to do so with less effort.

The other important thing to know about this concept is that our natural flow of energy doesn't necessarily look the same throughout our lives; that wouldn't make sense given the fact that we are constantly changing and growing. As we change and grow, a new "layer" of our Blueprint appears, especially when encountering big life changes, such as becoming a parent. What you naturally flowed or vibrated with before being a parent is very likely to change, and change drastically at that. Therefore, working with your Energetic Blueprint requires being willing to re-evaluate from time to time, especially around those big changes, and giving yourself permission to adapt.

In working with my clients over the years, and observing this phenomenon, I've noticed that people who have the most difficulty dealing with change are often neglecting to do the following:

a) Acknowledge that we are constantly changing, ever-evolving beings;

b) Acknowledge that life around us is constantly changing, and;

c) Acknowledge that it is necessary to adjust our expectations, habits, intentions, and support structures when encountering these changes.

When we do all of the above it makes it vastly easier to stay in the flow, maintain our alignment, and live authentically, and it takes out much of the discomfort that so often accompanies change. Conversely, when we don't take the time to do the above, we find ourselves meeting more resistance than is necessary and the discomfort is palpable, even painful. It may even appear as if we have detoured or created a delay in our paths, though I do believe this is ultimately impossible, as life is always working for us.

Some People are Our Energetic Matches, Some Not so Much

I'm sure you've noticed by now that in life we jibe well with some, and others, maybe not so much. That's putting it nicely, but you know what I am talking about. We live in a world with over 7 billion people and we're not going to instantly love each person we come across. Yet, as stated before, each person with whom we do cross paths most definitely serves a purpose in our lives, as we do theirs; it's just the packaging that might look a little different.

However, in terms of this Energetic Blueprint concept, there are basically three types of people we encounter throughout our lives: those we seem to naturally *flow with* instantly without any hard work at all, those that maybe do require a little effort, and those who we almost feel repelled by. I refer to the former as "energetic matches," or those that match our vibration to a high degree, and the latter as "non-energetic matches," or those whose vibration is simply very different from ours. The "in-between-ers," or the ones that you kind of like but maybe don't feel that resonant comfort and familiarity around are energetic matches to some degree.

What's important about this knowledge or perspective is that it has the potential to neutralize a ton of energy output that isn't necessarily in alignment with Who You Really Are. For me, it takes the sting and judgment out of human interaction when I happen to come across someone I don't like. Instead of getting into the drama energy of "Geez, that guy's a jerk. What's his problem?" I can simply acknowledge that we are not energetic matches in this lifetime, and therefore don't really need to "play together" this time around. This knowledge helps me to move on without my own mood or vibration being negatively impacted.

On the other hand, recognizing one of your energetic matches can lead to very rich and satisfying interactions. To put it in everyday terms–surround yourself with like-minded people and you will be uplifted. While that is kind of common sense these days, utilizing this Energetic Blueprint knowledge can be very useful on your road to success in any endeavor because it takes you a bit deeper. When I find an energetic match, I want to spend as much time with them as possible because being around them naturally brings me closer to Who I Really Am. When I am there, I feel limitless.

My husband is one of my purest energetic matches, and I wouldn't even say we are like-minded, at least not in the sense of this spiritual stuff. Yet we flow together so well, being together is absolutely effortless and deeply satisfying, and we naturally bring out the best in one another. Your energetic matches don't necessarily need to be the same as you in every way; it's more of a vibe thing. It's almost as if your energy fills in the gaps of the other and raises you both to a new level.

Bottom line: it's important to be aware of how you are feeling in every situation. If you feel good easily around someone, then you can trust that she is your energetic match and being in one another's presence will only propel you forward in the direction you say you want to go. If you don't feel good around someone, silently bless him on his path and move along yours; there's no need to make anything else up about it. But keep in mind that this, too, may change over time. In other words, someone who was your energetic match early on in life may not be so at some point, at which time you are faced with a choice: force it along out of obligation or give yourself permission to let her go with gratitude for the role she played.

Energetic match or not, you can be grateful for each and every person you come across in life, as well as every interaction you have. Because, at the very least, you are given yet another opportunity to decide, create, declare, and express Who You Really Are. Recognizing your matches and non-matches invites more awareness, consciousness, and intention, and it also allows you to disengage more easily from behaviors and aspects that simply aren't you. It makes for a cleaner, brighter, fulfilling, and more enjoyable experience altogether.

Our Superpowers

The last piece I'd like to offer as you begin to identify the components of your own Energetic Blueprint is the awareness that part of our Blueprint includes each of us having superpowers. No, really, actual superpowers. Perhaps not the ability to fly, have x-ray vision, or freeze everything with your hands, but powerful and amazing powers, nonetheless. The thing about our superpowers is that most of us don't realize that we have them, and if we do happen to notice we are good at something we fail to see it for the awesome and unique asset it is.

Along with my chameleon superpower and the ability to see auras and energy, I was alerted to one of my more subtle superpowers at a younger age. When I was in the 10th or 11th grade, my best friend's mom bought me a really pretty, soft, pastel-colored sweater for my birthday. She told me she chose it because it reminded her of me, in that it was very calming and made her feel good to look at it. She went on to say that I seem to have a knack for calming the space and the people in it just with my presence and I didn't even have to say anything. Aside from being incredibly flattered that this woman, who was not really known for doling out compliments, said such nice things to me, it turned on a light bulb inside of me. It made perfect sense when I thought about it, as I had noticed for quite some time that my friends all seemed to come to me for advice or just to be reassured about something. Even when my parents were going through their divorce, I was the unintentional "peace-keeper," despite being the youngest of four siblings.

I took this observation from my friend's mom with me as I moved forward in life. It even influenced my decision to go into a people-helping field like Child Psychology, and gave me confidence whenever I found myself to be in a position to assist someone. Now, in the present day, I use this intentionally all the time. I may not have the same degree of ability as Jasper in the popular movie, *Twilight*, whose special vampire power is to influence the mood of the people in the room, but I can calm the most frantic person down, if I do it right (that is, I am calm myself).

As I explore this concept further, I notice I am getting pretty adept at recognizing superpowers in other people almost instantly. A client of mine, who is also one of the coaches I have trained, has the superpower of extreme compassion and creating a loving space for people. When I was supervising some of her client sessions, I observed and felt these gifts, and much of the feedback the clients gave were about how loved, held, supported, and safe they felt.

My husband's superpowers include his unrivaled wit, humor, and easy-going energy. He can diffuse any tension with a quick quip that instantly makes others relax and smile, and I have seen him get a whole room of his aunts and family roaring with laughter with what I felt was not even his best work. People just love to laugh around him and he doesn't even have to try. His superpowers are huge assets to me and are largely what attracted me to him in the first place. There is no one on this planet who can ground and center me when I am falling apart more than that man. He reminds me of how simple life really is, and to just relax. I don't think he has any idea how valuable his skills are.

My mom has the superpowers of childlike wonder, silliness, and extreme joy. I have heard her be referred to as both a hummingbird and a fairy several times from various people over the years. Her energy is delightful and contagious, and she is unafraid to look like a fool. People get the most ridiculous smiles on their faces when they are around her, and tend to giggle like little school children. And boy, do kids love her; her superpowers include being especially good with them. They seem to recognize something in her that immediately puts them at ease.

There are obvious superpowers that go beyond the perceived ordinary, such as having strong intuition, psychic or healing abilities, and reading energy and auras. Yet there are countless other superpowers I've noticed that you might not immediately think qualify as such. Some of these include the ability to really listen and see others, having flexibility in thinking and living, the gift of story-telling (my dad had this one), the ability to influence others intentionally, having a giving spirit, possessing high leadership, writing and speaking abilities, maintaining eternal optimism and open-mindedness, being an exceptional cook, or having an extraordinary amount of passion and compassion.

Even someone's laugh can be a superpower. My sister-in-law has such a great laugh; it's delightful and makes you feel like you are a brilliant comedian. Or, being highly intelligent with the ability to convey that intelligence to others in a way that will help them understand–that's my friend, Arlene, who recently acknowledged this is one of her superpowers.

None of these things is small by any means, despite what you've told yourself about their commonness. What makes them superpowers vs. just a characteristic that many people have is that they come effortlessly and naturally to the individual, they don't even have to think about it and may not even notice it, yet it tends to inspire a whole lot of goodness and feeling good in others. It contributes greatly to the space. When you bring consciousness and awareness to these elements of Who You Are, you can begin to intentionally use them for even more good.

Practical Application:

Let's begin to identify some elements of YOUR Energetic Blueprint, shall we? Remember, bringing consciousness and awareness to these natural and soul-intended aspects of yourself has the ability to reduce the amount of resistance you feel at any given time. This keeps your vibration raised to such a level that makes it easier to access and be Who You Really Are. Know yourself and you will know how to live.

This is by no means a comprehensive list, but start by answering the questions to the best of your ability below, in your journal, and be on the lookout for more things as you let this concept sink in further. This is an on-going process of self-discovery, and it is really useful to do this with someone else, such as a coach, who can help you see what you yourself aren't necessarily seeing. I've added some possible answers to help get your brain moving.

Once you have awareness of these things, work towards honoring them in your daily life. That is, make your choices based on this knowledge of yourself to create more ease and flow. Fill your space as much as possible with the things and people that you naturally vibrate with, while doing your best to avoid, without judgment, the things and people that you don't.

My Energetic Blueprint

<u>My Preferences</u>: **In the categories below, identify some things that you naturally gravitate towards, as well as things that you find yourself repelled by. Feel free to add your own categories as well.**

Home/Environment: I prefer geographic regions where all four seasons are present and experienced, yet I recognize that winter is time where I tend to hibernate more and summer is time for movement and being social. I am drawn to warm or neutral colors, and anything that creates a cozy ambiance is good. I don't do well with a lot of clutter, and prefer open, clean spaces.

Social Life: I like a lot of downtime. I dislike my schedule being too full and too busy, and I detest being overcommitted or saying yes out of obligation. I prefer intimate and cozy vs. crowded and loud.

Work/Career: Working a nine-to-five job for someone else makes me feel like my soul is dying and I am suffocating. I need a lot of freedom, flexibility, and variety, and I have to be my own authority. Anything less is unacceptable. I have always been drawn towards anything that involves helping others, especially in the form of teaching and demonstrating.

Family: I am at my best when I have ample amounts of quality family time. I like closeness, both in physical proximity with my immediate family as well as geographic proximity with my extended family. I absolutely love and cherish family time. I am clear it greatly contributes to my alignment, and when I don't get enough of it I feel depleted.

Spirituality/Religion: I resonate the most with teachings that are marked by limitlessness and possibility, and are rooted in love. I buck against anything that imposes rules or requirements.

*Other Categories/Areas of My Life: These can include anything, no matter how small, such as "Food," "Clothing," "Hobbies," etc.

My Energetic Matches: What types of people do you enjoy being around the most and find are easy to be around? What types of people do you not enjoy and find are difficult to be around? Since this is your private journal, feel free to even identify specific people in your life.

Matches: I prefer down to earth, real people who are comfortable in their own skin, are confident, flexible, open-minded, and appreciate good humor, irreverence, and wit.

Non-Matches: I do not prefer people who are false or superficial, and who have no sense of boundaries or respect for others.

My Superpowers: What are you really good at? What comes naturally to you? What are your strengths?

I am really good at creating a sense of calm and ease, adapting to new or unfamiliar situations, and reading the energy of the space and of other people.

CHAPTER 15
YOUR ENERGETIC SIGNATURE

"Practice being appreciative, joyful, light, calm, confident, centered, beautiful, smiling, and knowing. These are attributes of the higher self."

~ T. Harv Eker

Much like we all have an Energetic Blueprint, which holds the secrets and details of how we naturally flow and move as energetic beings, each of us also has an *Energetic Signature*. An Energetic Signature is the path we are leaving behind us and paving before us, so to speak, as a result of the quality and focus of our daily thoughts over time. For example, if we spend most of our day focused on the negative, complaining a lot, and expecting the worst, we are practicing a specific level of vibration–in this case, not a very high one. When continually practiced, our Energetic Signature is created and becomes our *default dominant vibration*. In other words, when we are not paying conscious attention to the quality of our thoughts, the most familiar or "practiced" thoughts will take over automatically.

This is how we tend to draw the same experiences over and over and find ourselves in repetitive circumstances throughout our life. The truth is, the majority of people in the world have never been taught a thing about the conscious management of thoughts and emotions, not to mention vibration; so finding the same patterns showing up is very common. Until we come across a concept and technique such as this, the pattern will not be interrupted and the resulting experience continues. Your Energetic Signature, at any given point in time, even becomes what you are known for.

Think about it this way: Say you are bringing a new friend to a party full of your current and old friends, and are describing each person to this new friend to familiarize them before arriving. As you focus on the description of each friend, you find yourself generalizing things about them. "Jennifer is super upbeat and happy, and always has something interesting to say," "Erin is your go-to person if you need advice or insight on any topic. She seems to know everything about everything!" or "Try to avoid Carl, he is such a downer." What you are describing to your new friend, perhaps without even realizing it, is the Energetic Signature of each of these people. The very reason you are describing them this way is due to the vibration each of them is dominantly emitting, and it's what you and everyone else who knows them sees the most about them.

These are all hypothetical examples, of course, but let's take a closer look at poor Carl. Being described as a "downer" is indicative that Carl probably spends the majority of his focus on things that are upsetting, negative, or lacking in his life. He probably doesn't even realize he's doing it; he has just become so used to placing his attention on such things that it has become automatic. He might even be surprised to hear someone describe him this way, yet upon paying attention to *what he's been paying most attention to*, he would quickly begin to understand why that is. Although it would, perhaps, be a jarring realization, it would also be an opportunity for Carl to begin changing his Energetic Signature by changing his thoughts and what he is paying attention to. In no time at all, he could have a new Energetic Signature similar to Jennifer's!

Consciously creating your Energetic Signature is a far more fulfilling experience than succumbing to a default one that isn't your preference, or an accurate representation of Who You Really Are. Once you begin to engage in this natural process with intention and awareness, it can be fun and extremely satisfying. It is a very direct way to experience one of the highest truths of our being: We are all conscious co-creators, quite capable of creating any experience of life that we desire. We have all been given the tools in which to consciously create, the focusing of our thoughts and vibration being among the most powerful. Being aware of and intentionally writing, so to speak, your Energetic Signature is an effective and easy way to use these tools.

A Shower of Inspiration

When I first received this concept and insight, I was very excited by this fresh, new way to manifest and be in the driver's seat of my day. It came about at just the right time, when I found myself struggling to sleep well at night, wake up with gusto, and have enough energy in my day. This wasn't just one of those weeks where I found myself having a difficult time with this. It had been going on for months without me really paying attention to it and recognizing it was a product of my own thoughts and the story I was telling myself.

Eventually, I began to notice that I was enjoying my days less and less, and was having a hard time accessing the excitement and joy I had been used to, living the life of an entrepreneur who worked from the comforts of her home.

I found myself feeling stressed and overwhelmed in a job that typically had never felt like work, and housework and relationships seemed like more work than usual as well. I observed that I was "working for the weekend," a common syndrome that I had stopped participating in years ago. It wasn't long before I realized that I, a teacher of thought and vibrational management, had unwittingly created an unwanted dominant vibration! Sigh. It happens.

The concept of Energetic Signatures came to me in the shower, which is where I get my best ideas, inspirations, and "divine downloads" of information. This one was loud and clear. I don't always write down or act on what I receive in those moments, but this one had me running naked to my laptop (when will I learn to bring it in the bathroom?). I was in awe of the unfolding of it, too, as it was my very discomfort in realizing the pattern I had created that gave birth to a strong desire for something better, and voila, here I was given the means in which to bring it about! I went to work creating my new Energetic Signature immediately.

First, I began paying attention to the thoughts I commonly had each evening before going to bed and each morning upon waking, and it was there that I realized how I had let this happen. I was already adept at consciously making my first and last thoughts of each day ones of gratitude and appreciation, a habit I had picked up from the late, great Wayne Dyer. Yet I had gotten lazy about the thoughts in between. I would get out of bed saying my usual, "Thank you, thank you, thank you," but without noticing I would then allow my attention to fall on how tired I was, or how many times my youngest daughter woke up that night, or I would begin wrestling with the idea of going to kickboxing that morning while feeling so tired. My thoughts would then get influenced by the morning moods of my daughters, which were hit and miss, and if they were whiny, I felt whiny. The foundation I had laid for positive thinking through my gratitude practice was overridden by my attention to "what was" and the energy I was giving to it by talking and thinking about it all the time.

That leads me to the second part of my work around this: paying attention to the story I was telling about sleep and energy. I was aghast to find that I actually complained about it a lot. I think I was blind to it because I knew myself to be a positive, intentional person who didn't really complain much about anything, and if I ever did, I did so with purpose, consciously choosing to "go up" from there. Not with this topic, though, evidently.

So I had two things to work on: be intentional with the thoughts that followed my gratitude in the morning, and change the story I was telling about the topic altogether. In other words, no more complaining! When asked by my husband how I had slept the night before, I began replying with, "Gets better every night!" or "Very well, thank you," even if that had not been the case. More significantly, perhaps, I became diligent with the story I was telling *myself* about sleep and energy. If I caught myself thinking such things as, "I had better lay low today because I didn't sleep well last night," I would replace it with a thought like "I have all the energy I need and want today."

I began to rewrite my Energetic Signature, and as a result my experience of sleep and energy began to change. Soon enough I was sleeping more deeply with less interruption (even my daughter was sleeping better, imagine that!) and waking up feeling energized and motivated for the day. I even began getting out of bed earlier than I needed to–*voluntarily*. If you know me personally then you know what a big deal that is. Life returned to its usual level of vibrancy and quality, stress levels decreased, and my perspective shifted to knowing I had access to all of the energy in the world.

You Have More Than One Energetic Signature

The other thing I am learning about this concept is that we have more than one Energetic Signature. We have our *General Signature*, which expresses the totality of our vibration, and we have several *Subset* or smaller Signatures for the various topics and contexts of our lives. The personal example I just gave would be considered a subset Energetic Signature, as it pertained to the specific topics of sleep and energy. An example of a General Signature would be more like the hypothetical examples I gave above about Jennifer, Erin, and Carl. It captures the standout elements of a person's overall "being-ness."

As with our Energetic Blueprints, our Energetic Signatures change throughout our lives. As we are exposed to new experiences, ideas, perspectives, and external stimuli, the quality of our thoughts changes. As we grow, evolve, and expand throughout the various stages and phases of life, the things that hold our attention and focus change as well. In general, what people focus on when they are teenagers is not the same as what they focus on when they are in their thirties with a family and a full-time career. A particular stage, phase, or new experience in and of itself does not determine whether our Energetic Signature will be one that leans towards the positive or the negative–it is our thoughts, habits, and focus at the time that do.

We are all capable of consciously changing, creating, and impacting any Energetic Signature we hold, including our general signature. We can do this through awareness and focusing of our thoughts, emotions, and vibration, which takes commitment, consistency, and discipline.

By bringing awareness to our inner dialogue, we can determine the cause of our experiences and, if we desire to, seek to change it. And we can do this at any stage in life, no matter what our experience has previously been. If you're thinking right now, "Boy, I sure wasted a lot of time with a crappy Energetic Signature," I encourage you to let that thought go right now or change it to a better-feeling one. Because everything that happened prior to this moment of you reading these words are the very things that brought you here in the first place. Like everything in life, it served a higher purpose.

Life is always working for us. In All Ways. And now you have this great new tool to start working alongside life rather than against it.

Practical Application:

Let's get to work changing your Energetic Signature right now! Why wait?

I recommend starting with a subset signature so you can see the changes more easily, but feel free to go the general route if that calls to you in this moment. Decide what you are going to focus on and follow these steps:

Step 1: Notice the dominant thoughts you tend to have, either in general or regarding a specific topic. Are they good ones or bad ones? Are they limiting or freeing?

Step 2: Notice the story you are telling (to yourself and to others) about yourself and your life, or about the specific topic you identified in Step 1. What are you saying about it? How often are you speaking about it? Does what you're saying about it match your desired experience?

Step 3: Begin to make the appropriate changes. Start by actually writing out your new desired Energetic Signature, and read it out loud every night before you go to bed and each morning upon waking. Use a "key phrase" from it to help ground and connect you throughout the day, keeping you aware of, and intentional with, your thoughts. Hear yourself saying things that match this vibration to others, and to yourself. Be absolutely committed to it, knowing the energetic magic you are creating by consciously participating in your own vibration.

Example:

"Thank you, thank you, thank you. It feels good to feel good. Life is good. Life is always unfolding perfectly for me. Things are always working out, oftentimes better than I expect and in ways that surprise and delight me. My life feels lighter and lighter each day in every way. I love that I am in charge of my experience, my reality. I love feeling good. I love having support. I love Life and Life loves me, as evidenced by the countless amazing things I have, see, and feel every single day. Thank you, thank you, thank you."

Grounding/connecting key phrase: **It feels good to feel good.**

CHAPTER 16
SANTA CLAUS DOES EXIST

"I'm realistic. I expect miracles."

~ *Wayne Dyer*

I want to talk about miracles, magic, and manifestation for a moment. This might be my favorite subject to talk about, not just because of its enticing nature, but because I have believed in magic my entire life. I was fortunate to have that belief supported by both my delightfully whacky, spiritual mom and my logical, linear, yet open-minded and highly imaginative, engineer dad. They both in their own ways kept me pointed towards the magic and wonder of life. My mom was the one who exposed me to a multitude of spiritual schools of thought and perspectives, including that of the existence of angels, spirits, psychics, and healings. She also had an affinity for making all of my childhood events, like birthdays and holidays, magical and special.

My dad was not so much a fan of my mom's interests but he did not interfere with them. Although he didn't speak to me of angels and fairies and spirit guides, he took on the important role of pointing my attention to the magic of the Universe, of life in and of itself. He got me excited about the stars, space, and that special wonder you feel when you look up at the night sky and consider that there is way more to life than you can see. He had such a curious nature, and was not arrogant enough to think he had it all figured out; in fact, he didn't even appear to have a need to. It was enough for him to just be amazed by the simplest wonders of nature, of the evolution of life itself. He loved *The Hobbit* and *The Lord of the Rings* books, any tale of fantasy and wonder, really, and made sure to share them with my siblings and me at a very young age. He had a unique way of viewing the world that was based in both hard science and imagination, with plenty of room for curiosity and wonder. Put my mom and dad together and of course I believed in Santa Claus long after the appropriate age.

There was also the element of my ability to see and sense energy and auras, and often that would include seeing sparks of light, or these, sort of, vibrating "globs" of energy, and occasionally actual outlines of people who weren't physically there. I had my own proof of magic each and every day. I will say, however, that I was very picky about what kind of other worldly things I chose to participate in, and, especially as I began to develop my own belief system, I operated from the knowing that "it's only true for you if you say it is." In other words, as I grew older I didn't really have much interest in ghosts, and never once wanted to be someone who could see or talk to dead people, so I simply chose not to participate in that kind of stuff when my mom and siblings did. But angels, fairies, and Santa Claus? Bring them on!

Miracles, Magic, and Manifestation, Oh My!

When I work with my clients on the particular subject of miracles, magic, and manifestation, the main components we cover are acknowledgment and claiming. Energy flows where attention goes, so if you give something credit and acknowledge it out loud or on paper, claiming its existence, you can bet your bottom dollar that the Universe will conspire to bring you more of it and it will become a real, functioning part of your life. I had noticed over the years a single commonality throughout all of my interactions with people who also believed or wanted to believe in magic: they would share a special experience that was beyond the ordinary, and then would immediately talk themselves out of it, eventually forgetting about it altogether unless the topic was brought up by someone else. For example, if I offered a personal experience, it was as if they had forgotten about their own experience until I spoke up, like it had been tucked away in a secret closet in their minds that rarely got to see the light of day.

Miracles happen every single day, in every single instant, and magic is all around us all of the time. It is only a question of where our attention is currently being focused, what we are acknowledging, paying attention to, and making real as we tell our Life's story. *Conversations with God: Book 1* captures this greatly by stating, "All you see in your world is your idea about it." One small shift in your perception and attention and your world can take on a brand new array of textures, colors, tones, and characters. This is such an important concept to bring into your awareness and integrate into your daily life, because this energy is one of the highest expressions of Who We Really Are–that's why we find it so darned exciting!

Therefore, the first thing I have my clients do is start acknowledging these occurrences as they happen, preferably by writing them down. Writing things down makes them more real, you see, and gives it a whole different level of creative vibration. Plus, there's the added benefit of being able to come back to it and see your "evidence," which allows you to start telling a whole new story about your life altogether. They need not be earth-shattering things all of the time; in fact, it may surprise you to see how much joy you can feel simply by pausing long enough to consider what a miracle it is to watch a flower grow from a mere seed, or to watch your toddler take her first steps. My rule of thumb is to acknowledge and write down anything and everything that falls under the descriptive categories of beautiful, amazing, serendipitous, synchronistic, awe-inspiring, warm fuzzy-inducing, miraculous, and magical—you get the picture.

When I have my clients do this exercise, or when I do it myself, I refer to it as a "Miracles, Magic, and Manifestation Log," or M3. I simply instruct them to keep a small notebook with them that they can easily take out and write in when one of the three occurs, or to use their smartphones if that's easier. They can also add it to their daily practices of journaling, gratitude, and powerful questions, which we will go into more detail on later, by simply adding another space to reflect on as many of the magical happenings of which they can think. There's no wrong way to do it, and you may even come up with your own unique way. The important thing is to bring these experiences to life so that you may begin to know them as *everyday common occurrences* and as your dominant way of life, versus knowing them as rare events that are easily dismissed as coincidences. When you do so, the Universe has no choice but to deliver more experiences and events that hold the same magical vibration.

The "manifestation" part of the M3 exercise is a little different and deserves an explanation all on its own. Clearly we are manifesting all of the time; we are attracting certain people, events, circumstances, and opportunities to us via the Law of Attraction, whether we are aware of it or not, and the types we attract are dependent on the quality of our thoughts and what we are paying attention to the most. When I use the word "manifestation" within this context of exploring the magic of life, however, I am referring to the conscious, intentional manifestations we experience. This concept also includes the acknowledgment that all of the good things that are showing up in your world are there, in part, because of you (you can go ahead and ignore the bad ones for this particular exercise–you're welcome). This is really about strengthening your *manifesting muscle* and building your confidence and belief in yourself as the brilliant, conscious co-creator that you are.

Manifestations come in all shapes and sizes. Some are really big and obvious, like getting the brand-new car you've had on your vision board, and some are smaller and less noticeable. I encourage you to look for and acknowledge even the tiniest of manifestations, such as someone holding the door open for you, getting that last parking spot in a busy lot, or randomly running into someone you were just making a mental note to call soon. And still, some manifestations are even subtler, involving a change in how you show up in certain aspects of life. These are often the most powerful manifestations, too.

For example, parenting has been hands down the most stretching, challenging, mind-blowingly expansive context of my life to date. It's also been indescribably fulfilling, amazing, and made me feel all "ooey-gooey" inside. I frequently use the phrase, "my heart feels like it's going to throw up" when speaking of my kids, which makes my father-in-law giggle at the image, but that's the best way I can describe it. Yet being a parent also makes me wonder from time to time if I am bipolar or have split personality disorder, because I can go from that heart-vomiting state of being to wanting to rip my hair out, frustrated and exasperated, in the span of 20 seconds.

Managing my emotional and vibrational state within this context has been challenging, to say the least. It is the context that has caused me to feel the most like a failure, like the least resourceful version of myself, and the most shame and guilt. But being the ever-vigilant, good-feeling seeker that I am, not to mention that my capacity to feel bad for any length of time has drastically dwindled in this work, I made a conscious decision to work on this from the first time I heard some strange voice that ended up being mine yelling at my infant daughter (I reaallyyy hate admitting that out loud, by the way). Instead of having my state of being be at the whim of whether or not my daughter was crying, breaking, or spilling something, or in the throes of a tantrum, I worked very hard to manifest an emotional state not only independent of that, but in spite of it. I wish I could say that I was able to do that quickly and easily from the moment I remembered I was in control of even that kind of experience, but alas, it took me awhile. Six years later and two kids in, I am finally decent at it. But this is largely because in the beginning I was more focused on what I was doing wrong as a parent, how I was not measuring up, rather than what I was doing right. Once I caught on that it was in my best interest, along with my family's, to give myself some credit for manifesting some pretty impressive emotional states, the more common and effortless of an experience it became.

Remember, the key is to place your attention on the miracles, magic, and manifestations that are always there and are constantly occurring; emphasize those instead of placing your attention on what you feel you are lacking. This is the biggest challenge most of us have when trying to manifest and attract the things we want in life, or the type of life we want to live. We tend to be more focused on, and have therefore magnified, our lack of experience, and the thoughts and emotions that accompany that, than we are on the good stuff of which we want more. Shift the scales even the slightest and you will see a difference. Tell a new story about the role miracles, magic, and manifestation plays in your experience and you will begin to start living a life that reflects it. That's why this is such an important practice to develop, and it is loads of fun, too!

Ho, Ho, Ho!

To conclude the discussion of this topic as well as to amplify this vibration for you, I'd like to share one of my favorite representations of miracles, magic, and manifestation–one that blew me away.

In 2013, my husband and I decided we were ready to begin trying for a second baby. After basically getting pregnant right away but miscarrying only five and a half weeks in, we were devastated and disheartened. I won't go into that story right now as it's a whole other topic, but one of the things it gave me was an invitation to let go of "the how" of moving forward and trying again and allow the Universe to take care of the details. A couple of months passed where I dealt with the emotions of the experience, and worked on just being happy and present with my life, not trying to rush or force anything.

One day I received an email from a friend of mine whom I had known since junior high, but whom I only kept in contact with over Facebook with fairly surface-level inter-actions. Her email was far from our ordinary witty, sarcas-tic banter exchanges online; she was actually writing to me because she said "spirit" had been bugging her to contact me for months, but she was too afraid I would think she was a whack job so she kept putting it off. She asked me if I was pregnant, or was trying to get pregnant. I had not broadcasted my early pregnancy and subsequent miscarriage to anyone other than close friends and family so she was not even aware that we had been trying. Oddly enough, I had taken a pregnancy test that very morning due to some strange symptoms I had been noticing, really just to prove I wasn't pregnant and get the subject off of my mind, and it had indeed been negative. But you can imagine how my heart stopped upon reading her words–that was just too much of a coincidence to explain away! I responded by telling her about everything that had happened, and she said, "Well, don't be surprised if it happens soon."

I went about my business after that, merely noting it as a cool experience and also excited to know that my friend was actually one of my spiritual peeps; I had no idea about this prior to her email. I'm not sure if I was protecting myself from disappointment or just really okay with where things were, but I didn't think or obsess about whether or not I was pregnant in that moment or if I would be in the near future.

A few days later, I found myself at a local psychic fair, just for fun. I chose to have a 20-minute "mini-reading" from the psychic I was most drawn to, and before I had even asked a question she said with a soft chuckle, "Your spirit guides want me to tell you that Santa Claus is real."

I burst into laughter, because the subject of Santa Claus was kind of an inside joke between my guides and myself. You see, I had a really hard time giving up the idea and belief in the jolly ole' fellow when I was a (cough) teenager. Yes, it's true, even when all of my friends had long since stopped believing, I secretly clung to it for much longer. Not necessarily the idea that the fat man squeezes down a chimney and brings presents to kids all over the world in one night, but rather the essence and magic of it, the belief that the whole concept had to come from somewhere. To give up that magical part of Christmas was like giving up a very vital, core part of myself. I was well aware of how stupid that would sound at that age, so the only person who knew of my extended belief was my mom.

In fact, one of the biggest reasons I was reluctant to let the belief go was because of a very magical experience she and I shared when I was probably 11 or 12 years old. It was Christmas Eve night and, unbeknownst to the rest of the household, she and I had happened to come out in the living room in the middle of the night at the exact same time to sit by the softly lit tree. I was secretly trying to catch Santa in action, of course, but I'm not sure why she was out there. We sat by the tree together, talking about the magic of Christmas and using a crystal pendulum she had that we sometimes used to talk to our angels, when this particular old-fashioned Santa Claus ornament caught both of our eyes at the exact same time.

Trust me, I KNOW how crazy and perhaps stupid this sounds, but we both saw that sucker wink at us! We both reacted at the same exact moment, so it wasn't just one of us trying to make the night more magical and special for the other by saying it out loud and causing the other see what they wanted to see. We sat there in shock, laughing at what had just occurred in delight and gratitude. In fact, from that Christmas Eve on we made it a tradition to meet each other in the middle of the night to try to recapture that same magic, though I don't think anything like that ever happened again. But this experience was largely why I continued to cling to this idea of Santa Claus existing, really using it as a representation that magic itself does exist. And when I finally let the Santa belief go, I was depressed about it.

I struggled with that part of Christmas each year of my teenage and even young adult years, as "reality" began to overshadow the magic I had experienced as a child. Even though the magic of life and this Universe were still a big part of who I was, I still had moments where I doubted it all and where I felt very alone. In fact, since I largely navigated my life through feelings, signs, and intuition, I found myself having a crisis of faith quite often.

It usually went something like this: a significant event would occur and I would look to my guides, angels, and intuition to show me the way and give me confirmation of my choices. If it didn't pan out the way I thought it would, I would be devastated and question everything. But I always came back to the magic, as I quickly found that living any other way just simply didn't work for me, even if it meant I would end up being utterly wrong and misguided. In fact, this is what happened with getting pregnant all 3 times. Instead of relying on good old-fashioned technology and science, I was looking for signs and prompts from the Universe to tell me if I was pregnant or not. So when I had that miscarriage, I was not only devastated by the loss of the baby, but because it appeared that the guidance and support I had been receiving about it was wrong; this made me feel so alone and kind of dead inside, wanting to retreat from everything I thought I knew about life.

When the words fell out of that psychic's mouth, "They want me to tell you that Santa Claus is real," I was blown away by how my guides managed to find such a simple, short sentence to capture everything I needed to know and hear. They weren't saying that the man in the red suit was real, they were assuring me that magic is real, and I can trust it. My faith was further restored when she next said, "So you have two kids?" looking at Sati, my then three year old who was with me. When I told her I just had the one, she smiled and said, "I sense another one." A week later, I took another test and was indeed pregnant. And that pregnancy developed into my healthy, beautiful, vibrant baby girl, Hazel. Miracles, Magic and Manifestations, indeed!!

Practical Application:

Decide how you are going to keep track of the miracles, magic, and manifestations in your life. Write about as many things as you can notice and acknowledge each day in your journal, titling that section "M3." Keep a small notebook with you, or type them in your phone as you go throughout your day. But do it every day, and remember, the seemingly small and ordinary stuff counts, too, and can pack the biggest punch. This is a re-training of your thoughts and focus, and as a result you will grow your confidence and belief in yourself as the powerful conscious co-creator that you truly are, engaging consistently with the magic that is available to you all the time. Watch your experience of the magic and wonder of life grow, expand, and multiply, and your connection with Who You Really Are and the Universe itself will deepen exponentially!

CHAPTER 17
YOUR COSMIC TEAM

"Insight is better than eyesight when it comes to seeing an angel."

~ *Eileen Elias Freeman*

So far you've heard me reference my guides and angels often, appealing to their guidance and influence in various situations. I would be remiss to not include this invaluable aspect of being Who You Really Are, because the joy of realizing and utilizing a team of unseen beings who exist solely to help you along in your human experience is unmatched by anything else. Doesn't the idea of having your own team, completely devoted to you and unconditionally loving you, available at all times, never failing to give you an answer (if you'll receive it) sound amazing? The confidence, certainty, trust, and inner peace this awareness has brought me has been invaluable, and I would so love to see more people taking advantage of this gift we've all been given.

About a month ago, I was really in a funk. I was aware it was yet another "Breakdown Before the Breakthrough," but it was a really long and uncomfortable one. Worse than I had experienced in years, actually. Because I had been around the block a few times with this process, I knew to surrender to what was happening and take care of my needs the best I could. I was feeling very introspective and knew that I didn't want to be around people, so the next Monday I arranged to be as isolated as possible for the entire work-week. This really helped me move through the Breakdown Period more gracefully–until Thursday hit.

Thursday came and I was just plain irritable and crabby. Furthermore, I didn't want to do *anything*, including my usual "Breakdown Period" moves of napping and watching endless hours of Netflix. By about mid-afternoon I was finding it hard to even put up with myself, and out of exasperation I yelled, "Do something, please!"

I wasn't asking this of myself, I was yelling out to my "Cosmic Team," or my guides, angels, and other unknown beings I believe hang around to assist me with life. And they answered.

In the midst of pacing aimlessly after yelling out to them, I found myself absent-mindedly reaching for my phone and dialing the number of the conference line for a Mastermind group of which I am a part. If you're unfamiliar with what such a group is, a Mastermind is a group of like-minded peers who provide each other with support, ideas, and accountability. I typically meet and share with this group of amazing souls each week. However, I had already decided earlier in the day that I was in no condition to contribute, yet I began dialing the number without even thinking about it. When I realized what I was doing, I decided to go with it, knowing it was my Cosmic Team directing me in answer to my little tantrum a few minutes earlier.

Even though I was convinced I was in no condition to contribute, I hadn't stopped to consider that I was in excellent condition to receive. That call ended up being the most powerful and directly helpful call I had attended since joining the group several months earlier. I was very vulnerable and transparent with these people I knew and trusted, and put everything I was going through all out on the table. They immediately began to move together in perfect harmony with the sole purpose of assisting me through it. Each suggestion, word of validation, or perspective offered was like music to my ears, and they lifted me right out of my funk and into a brand-new place of clarity, certainty, and conviction, the likes of which I hadn't felt in, seemingly, forever!

I felt so supported, not just by the Mastermind group, but also by my Team of wonderful and devoted angels, guides, and loved ones for guiding my hands to pick up the phone and join the call. I was so steeped in my own fog of thoughts and emotions that they just did the work for me, and I absolutely love when that happens. That "tantrum" was not an isolated incident, either; I speak with my Team nearly all day, every day, as they are now a highly functional part of my life.

Because I was raised the way I was, by my mom in particular, I have always believed in guides and angels. I always knew there were other beings out there that we couldn't necessarily see but could often sense, and we've all heard the personal testimonies and stories about divine angelic intervention. I could see energy and auras and saw the outlines of angel wings and sparks of light that I just seemed to know were my angels and guides. So I made a decision a long time ago that, right or wrong, I was going to adopt and live by the belief that spirit guides and angels do indeed exist, and that we are all supported and loved by them beyond our understanding.

Who is on Your Team and How Do You Meet Them?

There are certainly more thorough and comprehensive sources out there on the subject, but what I would like you to know about this, from the perspective of alignment and being Who You Really Are, is this: *if you wish to have your Cosmic Team be a part of your experience of life, then simply decide that it is so and begin placing your attention there.* Acknowledge every little thing that you believe is an interaction or evidence of their presence. It is no different than with the Miracles, Magic, and Manifestation tool. The more energy and attention you put in their direction and the more you acknowledge and claim what is happening, the more interactions with them you will both call forth and notice. Don't waste any time wondering or questioning whether or not an interaction with your Team has actually occurred. Rather, consciously choose to give the meaning to the experience that it is real. *Even if it wasn't, your vibration will respond to the thought and still bring you more of it.*

The beautiful thing about our guides and angels is that they are always there no matter what, whether they were called on or not, whether we even believe in them or not. They don't go away, and they need nothing from us, although I do believe they are absolutely delighted when we are aware of them and talk to them.

I've always found it interesting that people assume that God and "higher beings" function the way humans do, being omnipotent and omnipresent, yet also petty, overly-sensitive, and vengeful. That never made any sense to me. I don't believe that God has an ego, therefore, God cannot be offended. How could God be when He/She/It knows all there is to know about everything, and everything that is created is an extension of Him/Her/It? Do you get angry at your stomach when you have a stomachache? Do you punish your toe if you accidentally stub it?

Likewise, our angels and guides do not have egos, nor do they have any other human trait that would cause them to act or respond in a less than holy way. They are never angry or disappointed in us; they hold us with great unconditional love and reverence. I've often heard people joke about how tired and worn out their guardian angels must be having to watch over them, and although I know they are mostly kidding, I'm guessing there's a small part of them that isn't. I believe that our Cosmic Team members never tire, for they are the epitome of the purest, uninhibited, and unlimited forms of the divine energy of which we are all made. They don't have to balance being human with being divine; they just love to help us with that. That's why they're here!

Of course, I could be wrong about all of this, but as I've said several times over now, it doesn't matter. What you believe about life is what you will experience, so why on Earth would you not choose to believe in the existence of such beings, *and* believe the very best possible idea about them? So if this part speaks to you, I urge you to be light and playful with it, and go with whatever aspects serve you.

Interestingly enough, I have no idea how many beings are on my Team, or who they each identify as, though I do know of a few. As it happens, for them as well as for me, this is not important. But a close friend of mine pretty much knows all of the names, faces, and purposes of each member of her Team, which works really well for her. She has a plethora of interesting guides: a dragon guide, an old Indian Chief guide, her deceased grandmother, and even a unicorn! There was a time where I might have thought that was silly, but who am I to judge? Especially when I observe how well her life flows consciously working with these guides, and how happy she is.

If you feel it's important to specifically know each of your Team members, go about finding that out and/or making it up; I am guessing you could call them by any name you wish and they'd smile and answer in delight. Remember, they have no need to self-identify the way we do, though they may do so in order to make it easier for us to access them. But if you're more like me and are happy with just feeling and sensing the energy of who is who, that's okay, too.

But do talk to them, reach out, ask questions or ask for help, share experiences, even if you don't initially feel you are receiving a response. It is unlikely that they are just plain not answering you. It is likely, however, that it's one of two possibilities: either you're not in a high enough vibrational state to catch their signals, or they are answering you in a way other than the one you expect. So be open and unattached, and as with all things, get into alignment first.

The more you connect with your Cosmic Team, the more real and functional they will become for you. As I mentioned, I've believed in them my whole life, yet they have only become a part of my everyday landscape in the most recent years because I wasn't placing my attention there often enough and I wasn't always in a place to access them.

My client, we'll call her Maggie, was so excited when she heard this component was part of the Spiritual Alignment coaching experience. She, too, had always believed in the existence of otherworldly beings, yet she had no idea what to do with that belief. She had this idea that there was some sort of anointment process to go through in order to communicate consistently with them, that you had to somehow earn it. Imagine her delight when I told her to simply start speaking with them, aloud and often, and look for and acknowledge the responses in the various forms they can come in. She dealt with the vulnerability and uncertainty that can often accompany this experience like a champ, always choosing to trust that she was indeed receiving their guidance, but she just didn't know how to interpret it yet.

By the end of our six months of coaching together, Maggie was telling me about how her Team would often step in and take the reins on certain things. For example, she once told me that she was dreading attending a networking function for work and was in the process of figuring out how to back out of it, when she noticed she was grabbing her car keys and heading for the door with the intent to attend it anyway. She described it as "almost going unconscious yet being fully conscious," like she just wasn't paying attention to what she was doing while she was doing it. She ended up attending the networking event, and it was there that she met someone who hooked her up with her next job, one that matched the description of her dream career!

There is such great value in feeling like you have a Team behind you, rooting for you and supporting your every goal or desire. We all know that this game of life can feel lonely sometimes, which is why becoming aware of and utilizing your Team is so important. And not only that, they are a direct line to Who You Really Are. In fact, your Higher Self is on your Team! Talk to him or her often, ask he or she what they would do in specific situations you are facing. Ask him or her to give you a sign in a way that you would recognize, because after all, who knows you better than your Higher Self?

Practical Application

Decide whether or not this particular aspect of spirituality is helpful to you, and if you decide that it is, then consciously choose to believe whole-heartedly in the existence of guides, angels, and other unseen beings that are here to help. Choose to believe that you have a Cosmic Team of your own who are ready and waiting to assist you, and are looking forward to the interactions. Then, begin acting on your chosen beliefs by speaking out loud to them, reading up on the topic of angels and guides (I highly recommend Doreen Virtue for this), and actively looking for signs of their presence. When you notice something, write it down. Give it credit, claiming its existence, and watch your entire consciousness expand to fit these divine beings in to your everyday life.

Signs and responses can come in countless forms, but a few to be on the lookout for are number sequences, words on signs or billboards, songs you hear on the radio, things that come up in conversation, synchronicity and serendipitous occurrences, or themes that keep appearing in your life. I have a dear friend whose deceased mother constantly shows her a specific car, a Chevy Malibu, I believe, to let her know she's there. My friend will be driving around and all of the sudden will notice that Malibus are everywhere, and she instantly knows her mother is with her.

Just like anything else we've talked about, build and strengthen this muscle of noticing and communicating with your Cosmic Team, and it will indeed become very strong. You may even want to visualize having "meetings" with your Team, perhaps during meditation or as you fall asleep at night. Picture them sitting at a table with you, or in a spot that is to your liking, and ask them questions. Discuss with them the "top orders of business," if you will. Write down what you hear, see, feel, and think after those meetings, and dismiss nothing. Sometimes you will receive answers you don't understand until later.

CHAPTER 18

THE EXTRAORDINARY

IS ORDINARY

"When you dedicate yourself to transforming your inner world, your life quickly shifts from the ordinary into the realm of extraordinary."

~ *Robin Sharma*

O ne of my clients travels a lot for work. In one of our sessions she mentioned that everyone tells her how exciting that is, which made her grit her teeth and want to roll her eyes. She loved her job, but was getting tired of all of the traveling, and no longer found it to be exciting at all. She didn't want to quit her job but really wanted to change her experience of this unpleasant aspect, so we focused on shifting her perception of it. Her perspective at the time was that traveling was always the same, and what had once been an extraordinary experience for her was now ordinary and mundane. Through some digging, we discovered that my client had resistance to the word "ordinary" itself, as well as any ordinary experience, which was largely why she could never seem to sit still nor settle down in life. It was hugely eye-opening for her and even caused a bit of fear and overwhelm at the implications, but she decided to just get started on transforming her experience of "ordinary" in the context of work first.

Using some strategies and techniques geared towards being more present and mindful, as well as consciously giving meaning to things, we shifted her perspective to one that felt much better: not only can the ordinary be extraordinary, *the extraordinary is ordinary.* It was her own word play, and I remember she was so excited because that phrase just fell out of her mouth. I got excited, too, because I hadn't thought of it that way, either. She meant having extraordinary experiences doesn't have to be saved for unusual circumstances, nor does it have to be few and far between. *She was saying that she could choose to live her life as if extraordinary were the norm and that her conditions did not have to change in order for her to experience them as such.*

We put this new perspective to work, both of us setting out to see how extraordinary the "ordinary" aspects of her life really were. Armed with her new tools and perspective, she set out on her next business trip, where she got upgraded to a fancy suite unexpectedly. That had happened before, several times in fact, but somewhere along the line she had stopped acknowledging it as incredible. From that hotel room, she sent me the following email. I've reprinted it here, with her permission, because I think her perspective is so powerful:

"Hi Nova, I have just arrived in Chicago and am enjoying my beautiful hotel suite I've been upgraded to. The woman behind the front desk was delightful; she seemed to take such joy in seeing my delight in the upgrade, and whispered to me that she gave me the best suite available. I am now sitting in the living room part of it on a nice, white leather

couch with my laptop. Just now I paused to look out the window and saw that the snow is softly falling outside, in that magical, snow globe, sort of way. The classical music I have been listening to while working on tomorrow's meeting plan all of the sudden sounds even better, and this room feels even more luxurious, yet still cozy. Add in my favorite pajama pants, a glass of white wine and a beautifully lit room that is perfectly complimented by the coloring of the February dusk outside, and here I have an extraordinary moment that is not too far off from any other trip to Chicago I've taken. I am now simply noticing and being present with what's going on around me. And it's amazing!"

I had my extraordinary, ordinary moment the same day I read her email. It was a Wednesday evening in February, and my husband and I had just finished feeding the girls, in a frenzy. My two-year-old was teething and being very vocal about her discomfort, and my six-year-old was highly focused on upsetting herself with a random hypothetical story she was making up, and wasn't exactly open to hearing a rational perspective from us. We were both overwhelmed, tired, and irritated, and secretly counting down the hours until their bedtime so we could unwind with an episode of the show "Dexter."

As quickly as it started, the frenzy ended. All of the sudden all four of us were sitting down on the floor, Trevor flipping through books and naming animal sounds with our youngest and me working on a puzzle with our oldest as she giggled hard about something I said that wasn't actually that funny, which made me giggle with her. I looked up at Trevor and saw Hazel leaning against him, patting his arm with her chubby little hand, and it was in that moment that I couldn't imagine being any happier, or life being any more perfect. It was the most extraordinary pause in time, and I was filled with such love and gratitude for things being exactly as they were.

That is how it tends to go when you stop to notice the beauty in everyday life. For God's sakes, I burst into tears the other day looking at a Kleenex I had used to wipe snot off my little two-year-old sweetheart's face earlier, feeling so much gratitude over the privilege of being the one to do that. And watching my oldest put her arm around her younger sister while they watched a movie, showing such simple, yet extraordinary love for her, was almost too much for me to handle. I just chose to really see it, to access what was already there. Please stop me before I list about 742 more moments about my kids and husband.

You've had these moments, too, I'm sure of it. You've had a lot more than you've allowed yourself to notice as well, we all have. The reason we miss most of them, or hold the beliefs that our lives are not extraordinary, is because we rarely allow ourselves to be present enough to notice how incredibly amazing the simplest things in life really are. To really allow yourself to slow down long enough to take in how incredible and cozy it feels to be inside a warm, comfortable house (or hotel room, as it were) just by watching a beautiful snowfall outside.

I mentioned earlier the quote from *Conversations with God: Book 1*, "All you see in your world is your idea of it," and here is where it is exceptionally true. We've already driven that point home when exploring perspective taking, but think about it in the context of your life as a whole, or as Who You Are. Your life, and you yourself are extraordinary.

Every single step you take throughout your day, no matter your situation, is a miracle. The fact that your lungs take care of the whole *breathing-to-live thing* automatically is stunning.

There is so much we take for granted on a day-to-day basis, and I don't say that to make you feel bad or remorseful but offer it as the key to finding extraordinary happiness with things exactly as they are. That is the point, isn't it? Not to strive towards achieving goals or manifesting a bunch of cool, satisfying stuff–those are just perks. The point is to be happy in any present moment, simply because you are here and you can be. This is the very nature of Who You Really Are.

Tell Your New Story

Your old story was the one where none of these things existed, where your life was full of longing, wanting, lack, not enough, and loneliness. If you continue to tell that story, you will continue to miss out on what has been there all along. It's time to tell a new story about your life and Who You Really Are.

I asked my client, Dr. Corey Lewis, if he would share his experience with this concept here in this book. His story stood out to me because I distinctly remember what he said in the beginning of our coaching relationship, when I asked him what he wanted. He had said, "I want my life exactly as it is, but better." Here is what he had to share:

"The story of my alignment begins with the voices in my head. You know the ones. Not the crazy-person, voices of Gods or demons talking in my head, but the regular ones, the voices we all have in our heads. You know the voices I'm talking about because you have them, too. In fact, they are speaking right now, agreeing or disagreeing with each thing I'm saying. The voice in my head was my own. And it was angry and hurt. It was mad and sad, and it was loud and obnoxiously incessant, like that dumb, drunk guy at the party who won't shut up.

I had just gone through a painful divorce and the voices in my head were constantly replaying old arguments, running what I now call "resentment and regret tapes." There was a recording that kept playing over and over again in my head. Replaying old arguments, re-stating, and reinforcing all the reasons for why I was angry, sad, hurt, and victimized. "She left me. She is so mean. My family is broken. Everything I ever wanted just got destroyed. I'm alone. I'll never fall in love and be happy again. I don't deserve this." And so on, and on, and on, all day long, without rest, or breath, or pause, a constant litany of white noise, of anger, sadness, and victimhood. And on top of that, or underneath it, there were quieter voices of discontent, of blaming, of feeling angry and hurt.

Professionally, I had become like the other harried professors around me, stressed out and pressed for time, angrily focused on the administrative problems around campus and the failings of our students. I was politically focused on all that was wrong with the world, insane wars, suicidal environmental destruction, and inhuman levels of inequality. Sure, I wanted to fix things and make them better, or so I said, but in reality, I was mainly focused on the problems, not the solutions. I was focused on pain rather than pleasure. How can anyone be happy when their head is filled with angry voices? How can anyone be happy when they are continually reminding themselves that they have been hurt and victimized, and that the world is a messed up place?

The truth is they can't be happy when they are doing that. And the truth was I couldn't be happy either. I remember desperately telling Nova when I first began working with her as my coach: "I want my life exactly as it is, but better."

Outwardly I liked many aspects of my life, and I didn't really need much of them to change, but I needed and

173

desperately wanted to feel differently about everything. Fast forward a few months and I am walking across the university campus in a light drizzling rain. I'm watching people scurry to class, some with their heads down looking at the sidewalk, others lost in thought, or plugged into headphones. I look around at the redwoods soaring overhead, the blooming rhododendrons, and beautifully kept landscaping. And I find myself wondering what the other people are thinking as they walk along. Some look stressed, others angry, and some are quick to smile and look happy. Then, I pause and notice what I have been thinking, and it hits me.

Just a few minutes before this moment, and in fact all day long, my voice, the one in my head, has been talking, and it has been saying a constant stream of gratitude, appreciations, and inspired ideas.

"God, I love my job, I'm so lucky I get to walk around this beautiful place. That tree is amazing. I've got such great sons, they bring me so much joy. I love this light rain. I'm so lucky to be young and single. I've got a great family. I'm so excited about the new book I'm writing. I can't wait to see how much the students like the new class activity I have planned..." One thought after another, on and on, about any subject I could think of, about my life, the world, and the person in front of me. It didn't matter. I had become grateful for all of it. In just a few months' time, nothing in my outer world had changed, and yet I felt completely different about all of it. And curiously enough, once I had become so aligned and had come to love and appreciate everything about my life, without needing to change anything.... all those things that had previously seemed so "negative" began changing on their own."

Corey's experience brilliantly illustrates what happens when we make that conscious shift in perception to noticing the beauty, joy, magic, and love that is already present in our lives. Appreciation will always point you in the direction; gratitude will take you there. Mindfulness, stillness, pausing, and breathing will all give you access to your extraordinary life right now, and show you that it is all within the most ordinary parts. Your extraordinary life *is* your ordinary life, exactly as it is right now. Where and how you place your focus and attention in each moment, the perspectives you choose and the meanings you give things, are everything. They are what make you the conscious co-creator that you've been all along.

Perhaps it's time to stop denying this, to stop giving energy to that old story about why you are stunted, stuck, unhappy, hurting, afraid, or broken and instead focus all of your energy into the magic of life and Who You Really Are. Begin telling your new, extraordinary story full of beautiful, ordinary, everyday life things that have always been there, you've just been looking the other way. Tell this new story to yourself and others as often as possible, in as many ways as possible, and watch your experience of life, exactly as it is, become even better.

Practical Application:

Are you noticing a theme here from the past few chapters? Place your attention on these things, acknowledge and claim them as they occur, and watch them grow, expand, and multiply.

Make a list of all of the "ordinary things" in your life that become extraordinary when you choose to look at them that way. From your ability to breathe and walk without thinking, to seeing the beautiful colors or hearing the incredible sounds of the world, to having the distinct pleasure of enjoying the most amazing tastes and flavors of your food. Your list may also include the people whose presence in your life make all the difference, the conveniences of getting around easily in this world, or the fact that you can access nearly any piece of information from any part of the globe simply by swiping your index finger across a phone screen.

By starting this list you are giving your attention to all of the good that already exists, and therefore you are giving yourself access to it that you didn't have before. Make this a place to focus your attention daily and I promise you will see a difference in your quality of life nearly overnight. Access these things now; you don't have to wait until you've been given the diagnosis that tells you that you're on borrowed time, or the love of your life leaves you, in order to appreciate and notice these things. Do it now. Start the page in your journal with the heading, **My Extraordinary Life includes,** and list away.

To Summarize Embracing Your Spirituality....

- Embracing your spirituality means embracing one of the most fundamental components of being a spiritual being having a human experience: "The how" is not up to us. Our job is to know with clarity what it is we want, and feel good as often as possible. This keeps us in a high-vibrating resourceful state, allowing the Universe to take care of the details, as well as enabling us to catch the "delivery."

- Rest, relaxation, play, fun, and pleasure are the most efficient ways to "get the job done," or be productive. When we allow ourselves to feel good, we are contributing to a higher-functioning brain and a higher frequency in our vibration, making whatever it is we think we have to do much more effortless and enjoyable.

- Each of us has a natural flow of energy that we can choose to follow in any given moment or within any given context if we merely pause long enough to look there. There are things that we are intrinsically designed to be, do, and have, based on our soul's agenda for this lifetime. These intentional components of Who We Are make up our Energetic Blueprint, which we can use as a guide in life. Knowing what we naturally vibrate with helps us to experience more ease, flow, and empowerment, helping us to functionally be Who We Really Are.

- Miracles, Magic, and Manifestation are actually everyday occurrences in our world. When we acknowledge and pay more attention to them, our awareness of them grows and the Law of Attraction draws more stuff like it to us.

- We were not sent here to do it all on our own. Angels, guides, and other energetic beings do exist; in fact, we each have a "Cosmic Team" behind us, specifically devoted to assisting us in fulfilling our soul's agenda in this lifetime. The more we acknowledge, talk to, and use our Cosmic Team, the more we will notice their presence and assistance in our lives, and the stronger the connection will be.

- When we embrace our spirituality, we notice that the extraordinary is really comprised of what we previously deemed ordinary. The smallest of things become huge, and daily life becomes filled with delight, joy, presence, and peace.

PART 4:
STORIES OF ALIGNMENT

I'd like to take this time to give you some real-life examples of how using the concepts and tools in this book can provide a beautiful experience of alignment, and how aligning with Who You Really Are can impact your life. These stories are just a few samplings told from the unique point of view of those who have intentionally used this work to connect more deeply with their true selves. I find that stories do a wonderful job of helping us to integrate big concepts more deeply, as well as demonstrate what these things can look like in functional, daily life. In Part 5, we will look at some very specific ways you can immediately begin living a life of alignment, and being Who You Really Are in your own life.

CHAPTER 19
REAL PEOPLE TELL
THEIR STORIES

From Greg Kruger, friend and fellow student of alignment:

To me, alignment became this feeling of being centered, calm, and more aware and in control of my thoughts and behaviors. I often say that all these calm feelings allow me to be in my most resourceful state. Now in the beginning, these feelings, this alignment, was much more fleeting. It's like starting a new diet, exercise routine, or choosing to change a habit that doesn't positively serve you; it tends to be extremely noticeable and exciting at first. However, as I began facing more challenging life situations, I found that without focus on my success habits and meditation, it was easy to slide back out of alignment and into my old behaviors, feelings, and consequential responses. The great part was that after having 40 days of continued repetition of my daily success habits, I became very aware of when I would slip! Furthermore, I also became well aware of how I felt as I walked out my door each day when I did or did not choose to focus on alignment.

I remember a specific time when I was just feeling troubled and irritable, but desiring to really just let it all go. After three days, I remember specifically walking in my downstairs hallway and being overcome with these negative feelings, but being sick of them, and then stopping where I was. I had asked out loud, "What can I do to shake this? What am I going to do?" Without pause, I heard a voice in my head say "meditate!" It literally stopped me in my tracks. I actually answered out loud, likely because no one else was home, "okay.... okay!" Then I immediately went up to my office and meditated. The result was breathing, calm, focus, breathing, calm, relaxation, breathing...calm...alignment.

This moment was so powerful for me because it reinforced the power I have over whatever emotional state that I am feeling...at ANY time. It reinforced to me the connection to my higher self, the best version of me. It reinforced that with practice I was gaining a deeper understanding of how and when and what I could do to be in my most resourceful state; what I could do to be in alignment more of the time. Ultimately, I realized that the very events and situations that surrounded me in my life could and would forever be interpreted differently.

I realized that in life we will always encounter situations of all sorts of challenge and variety, and that the most important factor in those situations is me. From my most resourceful state, any difficult situation not only looks and feels different, but my responses and the outcomes improve! In other words, I now strive to look at a situation that might have led me to feeling anger or hurt in the past from an aligned state of mind and being, and when I do I can see beauty and positivity where once there only held pain.

Around the time of this realization, I came across one of my favorite quotes from Wayne Dyer: "When you change the way you look at things, the things you look at change." Discovering alignment, practicing it consistently day after day, feeling the slip out of alignment, deciding to choose to come back to alignment (even up to 20 times on a tough day), and realizing that my energetic state is what changes, not my life's situations, has transformed my life in ways that I could never begin to adequately express in words.

Alignment, to me, is connection with my true self, the best version of me. Alignment with who I am has created a connection with our source of life; call that Source Energy, Being, God, etc. Alignment has created a deeper, more powerful and positive connection with all those around me, as well as with the way I view and handle life on a daily basis. To me, it is the fundamental base that allows me to have, do, and BE whatever I choose in this amazing experience called life.

From Amber Lang, long-time friend and workshop participant

Focusing on my own alignment has given me so many miracles. My husband and I had been trying for a third baby for six and a half years. We let things happen on their own for the first year or so, then I started obsessing over becoming pregnant again. I started to think about how I was not easily getting pregnant and how maybe I couldn't have kids anymore. After years of this continuing, I had a conversation with Nova about releasing and allowing. I let go of the current thought process I had and decided I was just going to take care of me and do what I needed, and if we had more children it would be an extra blessing. Well, all it took was a quick two months and I was totally surprised to find out I was pregnant! Once I shifted my energy from resistance to allowing, it all came together, and I am so grateful.

*I have wanted an SUV for over a decade. I always have extra kids with me and love the space it provides. However, my husband has always preferred the more economical cost of a minivan—not my idea dream vehicle at all. About a year and a half ago, my husband was looking at getting a newer vehicle for the family and minivans were what we looked at. We decided on a "**really cool one**" and got a Chrysler Town and Country with all the bells and whistles. I actually really appreciated this vehicle and was thankful to have such an awesome van from my hubby. I was able to find this* *appreciation by applying some of the daily practices I had learned. Daily, I wrote down ten things I was grateful for, spent quiet time in prayer, and also wrote down five powerful questions. Having my dream vehicle had been part of those daily practices. Like magic, a couple of months ago my sweet husband surprised me with my dream SUV! I couldn't believe it!*

So, I had my miracle baby and my dream car manifested, but I guess I wasn't done there. We recently had some family move in with us and our home was perfectly full. In some of my daily practices I began to ask questions about how to make everyone in the home feel like they belong and fit in better space-wise. My husband and I had looked into remodeling our home, but after pricing things out we didn't see it giving us the best value in the long run. My hubby said we should wait as he just wasn't comfortable with moving forward with the remodel.

Although I held it together in front of him, I was really sad and internally was throwing a fit. After two days of this internal struggle, I remembered to let go again, trust my husband's instincts, and trust the Universe to take care of the details; when the time was right I knew things would work out. Just a few days after I quit throwing a fit, my husband called and gave me directions to a location he wanted me to go to. When I got there, my jaw dropped. What I found were eight beautiful acres waiting for a home to be built on it. This land was exactly what we had originally wanted in our forever home plans, and the price was an amazing deal.

We are currently in the process of building our forever home on that land, and it will have rooms for everyone in our family. I consider it a major blessing to have family in our home with us, and now we all have better space. This summer we will move into our new home and continue being grateful and thanking God for hearing all of my prayers and allowing these principles to work in our life. I am so appreciative and amazed by how focusing my energy in this way allowed such miracles to occur!

From Julie Boudewyns, Intuitive Healer, Reiki Master, and Spiritual Alignment Coach:

This past January and February were absolutely brutal for me. My intuitive healing business was EXTREMELY slow, and finances were a weight sitting on top of me while I was at the bottom of a swimming pool, each dollar taking every last breath I had. Just when I thought I couldn't possibly get any lower, my ability to channel stopped. I couldn't connect with Spirit or receive a message to save my life! This was my livelihood, how in the hell was I supposed to work my magic when the biggest part of it was not functioning?! I would love to tell you that it only lasted a day or two, but that was not the case. Days turned into weeks, with just a few appointments here and there.

When I began this alignment process and running my business as a solo entrepreneur, I knew whole-heartedly that no matter what I had to stay the course. This was a time to really put that to the test. My daily habits were a must, and I focused a ridiculous amount of gratitude for anything I came across. As I was taught, I made it my top priority to feel good as much as frickin' possible, even when staring at my nearly blank calendar. I tried to pay attention to any signs that were around me since my spidey sense was out of commission, and I noticed I kept hearing the word "transition." It was in songs, quotes I saw on social media, conversations with friends, and then the owls started appearing. In animal symbolism, owls represent transition; two owls took up residence in my back yard, I saw random videos of owls being posted on Facebook, a friend even gave me the gift of a stuffed pink owl, saying that for some reason she thought of me when she saw it.

Right then and there I knew the universe had my back. I stayed focused on all that I had been taught in my coaching and training with Nova, everything I preached to my own clients, and I kept surrounding myself with anything and everything that felt good. By March, the block on my channeling lifted and amazing things happened. I had written several powerful questions over those two months geared towards receiving new clients, and no joke, one by one they were showing up at my door at a massive pace! My connection with Spirit was stronger than ever; I asked for four new clients in a week and boom, four new clients appeared that week, and then another three the following week! The phone kept ringing, from appointments being made to gift certificates being sold. I was in complete shock and have never been so grateful in my life.

From Alycia Brun, client

Since vigilantly doing my daily gratitude, affirmations, meditation, and journaling, I have:

1. *Landed my dream job. When I was a freshman in college, an advisor sat down with me and asked me what I wanted to do with my life. I specifically told her that I didn't really know, but that I someday wanted to work at Hazelden, a treatment center in Minnesota. "Someday" meaning like when I was 40 and seasoned in the field. Yet here I am, by far the youngest addiction tech there!*

2. *Received my level two Reiki certification. When I first started researching Reiki, I was like, yeah... How the hell am I ever going to be able to do this? And then connections started falling in my lap! This is especially significant because Reiki has allowed me to channel way more easily for people.*

3. *Discovered my new goal of becoming a yoga instructor. I constantly asked my guides what I should do to raise my vibration, and I was given the same answer every time until I finally listened: yoga. Now **get this**. I've recently been overwhelmed with people commenting on how I'm always smiling, energetic, and happy. One day, I was leaving yoga when the owner of the studio stopped me and asked, "Are you ever not smiling?" I smiled and said no. She went on*

to tell me how she wants me to go through teacher training and teach at her studio! I told her how that was literally my dream, but I'm not financially in a place where I can afford it yet. She told me she's going to find a way to make it happen through scholarships and grants. What?!

I shouldn't be surprised by any of this since my affirmations are things along the lines of, "I am so happy and grateful now that I am a Reiki master." I don't think I fully understood how powerful these practices are until I started witnessing them unfold right in front of me every day. I still can hardly believe it.

Practical Application:

What is your own current Story of Alignment? Write any changes you have noticed in your life that have occurred since you have been reading this book and doing the exercises outlined within it… any synchronicities that have happened to you, any improvements in your life, any positive movements in your attitude, nothing is too small.

PART 5:
HOW TO BE WHO
YOU REALLY ARE

We've now reached the juiciest part, likely the part that grabbed your eye and had your soul nudging you to buy this book in the first place. This is what life is all about it, isn't it? We all just want to be Who We Really Are. Isn't it funny how those words, "Who You Really Are," don't need much of an explanation for you to know exactly what I am talking about?

We all seem to share this yearning and desire to be Who We Really Are, because when we are our true selves we are tuned into the energy that flows through all of life, the highest energy there is. It feels amazing. We are filled with peace, joy, and immense love and reverence for all life. Influential new thought teacher and author, Neville Goddard, better known as just Neville, has said that we are the closest to God in those moments. He said, "It is when your feeling of reverence is most intense, that you are closest to God. And when you are closest to God, your life is richest." When we reach such high states of consciousness and beingness, we have access to every single thing we could ever want, every answer to any question, and we get to enjoy the feeling of being home.

To me, the messages of *Conversations with God* have always said it best: "We are all One. All things are One Thing, and all things are part of the One Thing there is. This means that you are Divine. You are not your body, you are not your mind, and you are not your soul. You are the unique combination of all three, which comprises the Totality of You. You are an individuation of Divinity; an expression of God on Earth." (*Conversations with God, Book 1*)

Who We Really Are is God. Who We Really Are is Love. Who You Really Are adores and loves you, and loves everyone else, too. Each of us expresses this differently, of course, and it isn't even necessary to be all of Who We Really Are in order to experience great happiness and satisfaction. Neale Donald Walsh says, "Does my True Identity have to be experienced totally for my life to have meaning and to be fulfilling? No. I get that, too. I am clear now that attaining even portions or aspects of the Divine is sufficient for me to know immense joy and fulfillment."

The benefits of knowing and being Who We Really Are can be experienced from a more practical level as well. Gregg Braden, author of *The Divine Matrix*, says, "Knowing who we are is the basis behind every decision and choice we make. Knowing and being who we really are is the difference between being knocked down by extreme changes or circumstances and growing with them."

We have all had glimpses of Who We Really Are throughout life, some of us more than others perhaps, and I believe it is what we are all working towards in one way or another, even if some wouldn't describe it that way. The problem is, most of us were taught a few things that block us from the joy of knowing and experiencing Who We Really Are, making the journey a rough one at times.

Most of us were taught that we need things outside of ourselves in order to be happy and feel good. And many of us were taught that we didn't deserve happiness, or needed to earn it. Still others of us were taught that it's not even okay to be our true selves, and that we must conform to society's expectation of who we should be instead.

There's a lot of pain that comes with these beliefs, and seeking to align with your truest, highest, innermost self is the most direct path I know of to create healing, connection, and understanding, opening the door to a new way of life.

So how do you be "Who You Really Are?" In short, feel good more often. Anything that gets you into a high-vibrating state will get you there. The answer is simple, but you have to actually do the work in the face of life's endless distractions and objects of attention that only lower your vibration. What is offered in this section are some ways to make *feeling good more often* easier for you to accomplish.

I have given you a lot to absorb and put into practical use so far, and what I am offering to you on the following pages is essentially a guide to putting it all together. These are what I have found to be the most useful and effective elements of focus in this business of being Who We Really Are, and they are the ones I spend the most time on with my clients and within my own life. This approach derives from over two decades of study, research, observation, personal experience, and directly guiding others around this topic. It is by no means the only way; it is merely another way, yet one that happens to work really well for virtually everyone I have come across in my work. Try it and see how it works for you.

CHAPTER 20
DEVELOP A DAILY PRACTICE

"What you do every day matters more than what you do every once in a while."

~ *Gretchen Rubin*

Throughout this book you have often heard me refer to having a daily practice, or participating in specific daily habits. In my coaching practice, the very first thing I start a client on, whether they are with me for the long haul or just one or two sessions, is a set of daily practices they can commit to, and complete, each day. These are their highest priority. I stress to them that these practices are as important as eating, sleeping, and breathing–because they are. In fact, if a long-term client decides not to do their daily habits or stops doing them completely, then the coaching itself stops. Not because I'm mad at them or offended and outraged that they didn't listen to me, but because there's really no point in doing alignment work without these practices. At the beginning of my relationship with my own coach he put me on a set of seven daily habits and told me right off the bat that if I stopped doing them he would fire me and keep all of my money. He saw that my life was absent of these practices and recognized they were the most vital piece to taking me where I said I wanted to go. He knew our work together would be pointless without them.

Intentionally choosing to engage in daily habits that focus your thoughts, emotions, and energy in a positive direction is the single most effective and helpful practical tool that I am aware of for helping one merge with their Highest Self. As far as I am concerned, having a daily practice is the same as practicing the vibration of Who You Really Are. Over time, you simply become that.

You see, keeping a set of practices that you return to day in and day out are so effective in keeping you consistently in alignment because they allow you to show up consciously for yourself each day. They are ways of connecting with your soul and merging it more fully with your human self. They allow you to harness the energy that makes you a powerful force in this world versus letting it get scattered far and wide from all of life's distractions. Furthermore, they give you continuous access to all of the inspiration, resources, answers, clarity, and ideas that seem to elude us when we are stressed or just in a plain old bad mood (a.k.a. misalignment).

Again, misalignment was my main issue when attempting to gain momentum in the earlier days of my coaching career, and in my life in general. I wasn't seeing clearly enough often enough, and wasn't consistently making decisions or managing my thoughts and emotions from an aligned place. When I began those seven daily habits, I saw big changes right away in the way I operated from within. It was only a matter of time before I began to see my external world reflect these changes. In addition, my true self emerged and became my "usual" self more than ever before.

Each time I start a client on their daily practice and hold them accountable to it, I get to experience that shift I felt all over again through them because they begin to notice the changes immediately as well and are excited to tell me all about it. It never gets old.

The 3 Most Magical Words in the English Language

Being a spiritual coach, most of my clients have dabbled in meditation prior to working with me. Some were even consistent with it for a while here and there but ultimately did not have a disciplined practice, which is curious because they all say the same thing: they feel good, centered, and clear when they meditate. Yet for some reason they don't do it every day or even very often despite knowing the benefits.

This phenomenon is quite common, in fact. I suffered from it at one time, too. Before working with Dustin, I was a dabbler of sorts with a lot of spiritual practices but none with any kind of consistency, commitment, or discipline. When we began working together, I noticed having someone holding me accountable left no room for excuses or justifying to myself why I wasn't doing something I knew would benefit me.

It doesn't necessarily matter what your daily practice consists of; in general, it all comes down to what works for you, what you enjoy, and the fact that you do it every single day. That latter part is the one most people have trouble with, so the key is to choose habits/practices that bring you pleasure and are doable. If the elements of your practice meet those criteria, you will have less trouble practicing them consistently. Someone who may not define themselves as spiritual at all but takes part in gardening every day simply because they enjoy it so much is unwittingly experiencing alignment and being in the flow.

It doesn't matter what you do, the key ingredients are *consistency, commitment, and discipline*–three words that might make most people shudder and associate negatively, but used in this context, they are perhaps three of the most beautiful and magical words in the English language. A great example of this is the martial artist. A martial artist who practices once a week experiences a certain level of success in his abilities, as well as a certain amount of pride, joy, and pleasure. A martial artist who practices every day and works her butt off to become a black belt has a much higher skill level, and therefore experiences a much higher level of success, pride, joy, and pleasure.

Even though it doesn't matter what you do each and every day, there are a few practices that skyrocket you to your own alignment, ones that intentionally and directly help you get into your desired state of being more easily, and I'm going to share them with you here. My suggestion is that you do them all for at least two weeks straight, no matter what, and try to enlist an accountability partner. As I say to my potential clients, I don't care what you do beyond those two weeks, but give yourself that time to find out for yourself the value in it. In fact, I don't officially take a client on until they do this. Of course, it is my hope that you will continue to practice these daily habits (or some version of them) for the rest of your life, but 14 consecutive days is a good place to start and is doable, right?

If you only choose to act on one chapter of this entire book, I hope you'll let it be the following chapter. If you began to consistently implement these practices and nothing else I have offered, I assure you, it would be enough. This is one of the most consistent pieces of guidance I see amongst my favorite teachers and messengers out there: have a daily practice and, for the love of God, make it actually daily.

Neale Donald Walsch will tell you this, Abraham-Hicks will tell you this, Wayne Dyer, Brené Brown, Tony Robbins, and Eckhart Tolle have all said it too...the list goes on. These particular practices are downright magical, as I've heard my clients and others who have done them say again and again.

So, without further ado, I present to you...

Chapter 21
The Daily Alignment Habits

"Ego says: Once everything falls into place, I will have peace. Spirit says: Find your peace, and then everything will fall into place."

~ *Marianne Williamson*

Gratitude

I begin with this habit, because it is incredibly transformative. In fact, you may recall I already gave it to you in an earlier part of this book as a practical application for alignment. I simply couldn't wait until this final section, because it is so powerful and easy to adapt into your daily routine. Practicing gratitude and appreciation alone will change your life for the better in countless ways, and immediately so, because it is an instant perspective-shifter. It is also a strong "access point" to the God/Source energy of which we are all comprised. Remember earlier when I said if you only applied one chapter let this one be it? Well let me further narrow that request: if you only do one habit, let this be it.

Practicing gratitude is a big deal in the personal and spiritual development arenas these days, and is even beginning to eek its way into the corporate world. Vishen Lakhiani, author of *The Code of the Extraordinary Mind* and founder and CEO of Mindvalley, a publishing and education company that became one of the fastest growing private companies in the world, uses it as a fundamental principle of running all of the multiple branches of his company.

Mindvalley has won numerous accolades, including *WorldBlu's Most Democratic Workplace* and a certification by *Great Place to Work®,* and the company attributes its unique success to shifting the focus in the workplace to the happiness and well-being of their employees. Part of their workday includes daily practices, and gratitude is at the top of the list.

Gratitude is taking the world by storm because a) we are ready for it, and b) it is the quickest way I know of to transform an experience, or a person for that matter. It works, and the process is so satisfying. There is nothing better than thinking you don't have much good in your world, only to look a bit closer and see you have a ton of amazing things to feel good about. The Law of Attraction then steps in and does its thing, giving you even more to feel good about.

If you've been paying attention on social media, this gratitude wave has definitely had an impact. There are "gratitude challenges" all over Facebook and Twitter, coaches and authors are writing about it and creating programs for it, and every November you can find all of your friends posting something they are grateful for each day on the above social media platforms. Gratitude has become trendy.

While there are plenty of people around the world who are now aware of this tool and have even practiced it a bit, there aren't as many who do so with any sort of consistency. It's another one of those "I know it works and feels good but I just don't do it enough" phenomena. Yet if they understood the mechanics of how having a daily gratitude practice actually works and its benefits, they might decide to make time for it.

Again, the key here is consistency (you're probably going to want to slap me for how many times I am going to stress this point, but you'll probably thank me as well). On average, we each have over 60,000 thoughts a day, most of which we have unconsciously. Since thoughts are energy and are creative, that's a lot of energy not being properly directed, energy that can lead to a lot of anxiety-filled, chaotic, and confusing experiences. *Practicing gratitude allows us to focus a good portion of those thoughts in the right direction, to actually **re-train** our brains to function in such a way that helps us to create more positive experiences and interactions in our lives.* It is the very thing that can turn a "glass is half-empty" type of person to a "glass is half-full type," by building new neural pathways in the brain that make it easier and more natural to see the world that way. When one is looking at any given subject matter in a positive light, their experience of it becomes better because, put simply, perspective determines experience.

Focusing on gratitude makes us feel good and relaxed about ourselves and life, and remember, the brain functions better when it's relaxed. The conscious mind has access to more resources, ideas, and answers than it does when the brain is stressed.

Energetically and spiritually speaking, gratitude is the easiest, quickest, and probably most effective way I know of to raise your vibration. As with the brain scenario, when you are focusing on the things for which you are grateful, your vibration raises and all of the sudden you have access to the resources that support you in your life endeavors. You have more energy and motivation to clean your house, write that article, have that conversation, or finish that project. And by golly, you actually even enjoy it!

Focusing on what's already good in your life also brings you to the present moment which, if you've read any of the popular spiritual titles out there, you know is the only real moment that exists or matters. All happiness and good-feeling stuff exists in the present moment, you just have to find a way to step out of that train of 60,000+ thoughts a day that are focused on the past or the future in a negative or lack-based way in order to see it. Gratitude does exactly that. In any single moment or instance you manage to do this, you are said to be "in the flow" for a period of time. Do this every day and you will be in the flow nearly all the time. Doesn't that sound nice?

I am a fan of putting structure to your daily practices, as it helps support you in the whole consistency part, giving you steps to follow. Below is how I do it and how I instruct my clients to do it. Feel free to make adjustments as needed to better fit your own unique personality.

- Each day write out at least five things (ten is better!) that you are truly grateful for, no matter how big or small. I say "truly" because it is easy to go the route of "should." For example, you "should" be grateful for the roof over your head or the food on your table, but sometimes you just aren't connected to the feeling of it. I urge you to look for the things you can immediately feel appreciative of and good about, even if it's the comfy slippers on your feet, the sun shining through the window, or that a stranger smiled at you.
- Each night before going to sleep, after you've turned off the TV, put the book down, or turned the light off, consciously and intentionally make the first and last thoughts of each day be thoughts of gratitude and appreciation. Trust me, this feels so much better than going through your to-do lists in your head or

obsessing about what you didn't do right that day. And you'll fall asleep more quickly to boot! Energetically speaking, the frequency you emit as you fall asleep is the one you will wake up with, so if you do this you will wake up feeling good!

- Each morning upon opening your eyes, consciously and intentionally make your first thoughts of the day be ones of gratitude and appreciation. Even if you're not a morning person, simply open your eyes, smile, and say "thank you, thank you, thank you." For what? Who cares! You are setting the tone for your day, and this one feels much better than "Okay, I have to get the kids ready for school, make lunches, send that email..." Plus, in this vibration you will be able to do all of the above with more pleasure and greater efficiency.

Sometimes it can be difficult to access the energy of gratitude, especially if you're new to the concept or you're starting off from a lower-vibrating state. If the word "gratitude" or "grateful" makes you feel more resistant than good, try one or more of the following tips:

- Think of someone or something that is easy for you to feel good about as your subject for gratitude. For example, you can choose your children, and reflect on all of the positive aspects you appreciate about them.
- Mix up your language, reaching for words that feel better to you than "grateful." Sometimes phrases such as "I enjoy," "I appreciate," "I like/love," "I feel good about" are easier to access.
- If you're having a hard time coming up with five or more, try asking yourself what you're grateful for

or what you appreciate within the different categories of your life. What are you grateful for in your personal life? Your professional life? What are you grateful for about your health? Your family? Your strengths? Sometimes categorizing gets the brain working better.

That's it. Simple, right? Carve out time to do this and make sure you are writing them down versus just thinking them. Thought is creative, but writing a thought down is even more powerful and carries a higher energy. After doing this a bit (consistently, of course) you will notice how simply good it feels and how much more relaxed you are afterwards. Then, after doing them longer, you will notice that you not only feel good when you are engaging in this practice, but you feel good throughout the day, too. This is because your brain and your vibrations are now trained to tune into the gratitude that is always available to you, but that you were most likely not paying much attention to before. Your brain naturally begins seeking it out because it has been re-wired to do so. You tune into it more easily because it is your very vibration that attracts even more things for which to feel grateful and appreciative. Magic, I tell you!

Powerful Questions

This habit is far less recognized than gratitude, despite its seemingly self-explanatory name. In fact, if you're a coach or a therapist you may have the assumption that you know what this means. Yet this technique is far more powerful and effective than the name implies, and when you use it consistently with an understanding of what's really happening, it is downright magical. Using powerful questions, as a daily habit, is one of the most effective ways I know to apply, practically, the knowledge of our partnership with the Universe. If you'll recall from an earlier chapter, our job is to know what we want and feel good as often as possible, in order to stay in a state of allowing. It's the Universe's job to take care of "the how" of it manifesting. But before we go there, let's take a look at the technique itself, and how to use it as a daily habit.

Powerful Questions are positively-posed questions that feel really good when asking them, giving you a sense of relief, hope, joy, excitement, wonder, contentment, etc., and they are questions that you do not attempt to answer. The magic is in the asking, and the type of question you ask in any given moment or situation is largely responsible for the experience that follows.

We are constantly asking powerful questions in our daily lives. However, the majority of those questions are riddled with fear, doubt, anxiety, stress, worry, and even panic. Furthermore, we insist on trying to answer them from those less resourceful states of being. For example, have you ever heard yourself or someone you love say something like, "Why does this always happen to me?" or "What else can go wrong?" or "What if it doesn't work out?" If you are indeed human, I'm guessing you are all too familiar with that line of questioning. These are all examples of powerful questions because they take us somewhere, they define our chosen perspective and therefore impact our experience. Essentially, they give the present energy a direction in which to flow. In this case, these are negatively-skewed or posed powerful questions, so the direction in which our energy flows is going to be one that is probably *the opposite of where we really want to go.*

Go ahead and ask those questions above out loud, just for funsies. With each one, notice what is happening to you physically. Do you feel your stomach drop? Does your body hunch over a bit or become tighter? Does your throat feel constricted perhaps? That's because thoughts are energy, and when you direct them in a certain way that energy begins to flow immediately and produce physical responses. In other words, your body expresses the energy that is flowing, whether it's in a positive or negative direction.

As with the daily practice of gratitude, when you ask powerful questions that feel good, it raises your vibration and gives you access to more resources: more thoughts that match that frequency, more answers and opportunities that are in alignment with what you want, and the motivation and desire to take action. It begins to flow energy in the direction *that you say you want to go.*

Humor me again. Ask the following questions out loud and notice how you feel: "How awesome can my life get?" "How much love can I feel today?" "What if it all worked out perfectly?" Notice a difference? Again, assuming you are human, it is likely that you felt a bit of relief, of excitement, even. Perhaps you stood up straighter, or your muscles relaxed and you got a smile on your face. These positively-skewed questions took you somewhere good and you could *feel* it.

If you're well-versed in the personal and spiritual development world, I am certain you have heard the terms "limiting beliefs" or "old thought patterns," probably to the point where you want to scream the next time you hear them because you still don't know what the heck to do with them. Well you are in luck, friend, because cultivating the daily habit of powerful questions will quickly and naturally release and replace any old thought patterns or limiting beliefs you've had, and you may not even notice it taking place! In other words, there is often no need to sit and hash and re-hash our old stories to death with the aim of processing and eventually releasing them, when you can literally begin to re-train your thoughts by asking yourself better questions. Isn't that awesome?

Beliefs and ways of thinking we adopted from childhood or perhaps from a traumatic event do not stick around simply because of the event itself. They stick around because we keep repeating our thoughts about them and we continue to practice functioning from that place. It is habit.

For example, if you grew up in poverty and unconsciously formed the belief that there isn't enough and you will always be poor, you may find yourself in your adult life asking questions like, "Where is my next dollar going to come from?" or "What if I can't make the mortgage this month?" Those questions choke you with fear and panic, and attract more thoughts and therefore experiences like it–unless you break the pattern. To continue with this example, if you were to one day decide to instead ask, "What if it was all going to be okay?" or "How would it feel to always have more than enough each month?" or even "What needs to happen in order for my experience of money to be different?" then you would begin to pave the path for a much better experience of money. Your new thought patterns and beliefs would automatically replace the old ones over time.

I know some of you read that and thought, "Yes!" but I'm also guessing a few of you read that and thought, "Sounds nice, but is probably a bunch of fluff or is too good to be true. There's no way it can be that easy." To both groups, allow me break it down for you…

Ever hear of the colloquial definition of insanity? That it essentially means to do something the same way over and over again expecting different results? Being that thoughts are energy and become things, it is unrealistic to continually think a thought or hold a certain perspective and expect to experience something different. You need to do something differently in order to have a different experience, and that requires changing the thought first.

Do you remember how you felt a minute ago when I had you say the negatively-posed powerful questions out loud? That feeling was the result of your energy dropping, and when we are vibrating at a lower frequency, when the brain is under a lot of stress (which negative thinking causes), we no longer have access to the answers, perspectives, resources, ideas, and opportunities that would lead us to a more desirable outcome or experience. Therefore, the cycle gets repeated and nothing changes. For you metaphysical junkies, the Law of Attraction responds to the lower vibration you are emitting and sends you more of the undesirable stuff, thus the cycle gets repeated and nothing changes for the better.

Got it? Now, let's take a moment to entertain the group of you that said, "There's no way it's that easy." You're right. It's not easy. It takes (drumroll please).... *commitment, consistency and discipline* to implement this. In other words, if you expect to change your thought patterns, perspectives, and beliefs, you need to continually beat the same positive drum over and over again, which takes a lot of conscious effort. Hence, using powerful questions as a daily habit.

I always tell my clients that I wish I had the technology handy to take a picture of their brains at the beginning of our six-month coaching journey and one at the end so they could see the neurological changes that take place. I am certain it would look drastically different because that is roughly 180 consecutive days of thinking on purpose and in alignment with the person they want to be and the life they want to live versus how they've always thought before.

While I don't have the technology to take those pictures (what if I did someday? Ha ha), I do have the picture that is their life story, and how vastly different it is from start to finish over that six-month period of time. If their entire outer landscape hasn't visibly changed to the naked eye, you can bet their inner landscape has, and the outer one is quickly catching up.

Let's get back to the Universe's role in this habit. I've said that you don't attempt to answer the powerful question you pose. Why is that? Because that is the act of you allowing the Universe to answer it for you (feel free to replace the word "Universe" with "God" or any other word that better fits your language here. I like to use "Universe" as, to me, it is a simple way of representing All That Is).

Your only job after posing this positive-powerful question, and not attempting to answer it, is to feel good as often as possible, which again, keeps your vibration raised. This is what allows the Universe to deliver on "the how" of it; think of it as keeping the door open for the cosmic delivery man. If you're stressing out trying to control and account for every detail of something you want and are trying to force it to happen, then your vibration drops and the door slams shut on his face just as he is waiting to bring you your package. Fortunately, the cosmic delivery man is patient and just waits for the door to open again.

I can't tell you how many powerful questions I have written in my journal over the past four years that I have later watched come to fruition. That's really the exciting part here after you've been at it for a while; you begin to know with certainty that the very question your pen is crafting on paper is really an order you are putting in with the Universe, and it is only a matter of time before it comes to be. This feeling is indescribable, and allows me to relax into my life perhaps more than anything else, knowing I am taken care of.

One of my favorite examples of this occurring is when I have a spot opening up in my client roster, or I find myself in a business "ebb" and am wanting more fabulous people to work with. I ask the powerful question, "Who will my next ideal client be?" or "What if my next ideal client hired me within the week?" And sure enough, in no time at all, that spot is filled. Remember, I don't really make any effort in the way of marketing or seeking clients out, they just seem to find me exactly when I am ready for them. For all of you coaches and entrepreneurs out there, consider this my "marketing plan."

Now that you know a bit about the mechanics of this impressive daily habit, allow me to give you a more acute definition and a structure to practice it in:

Powerful Questions are positively posed questions that feel really good in the asking of them, giving you a sense of relief, hope, joy, excitement, wonder, contentment, etc. Once you write down the question, don't answer it. Allow the Universe to take care of "the how" of the question and answer it for you. Your only job after asking a powerful question is to feel good, as often as possible, so the Universe can deliver it to you. Neurologically, when you ask a powerful question, it causes a sense of relief and helps your brain to relax on the spot. This habit is training your brain to look at things in a better way, creating new neural pathways and thought patterns that serve you better than the ones you had before.

As a daily habit, it is recommended that you write down at least five powerful questions each day. These questions can be general, such as "How much love and joy can I stand today?" or specific, such as "What is one impactful step I can take towards financial wealth and abundance?" Powerful questions may be repeated each day, as long as the asking of it still evokes a positive feeling or response. If it doesn't, re-word the question in a way that does, or ask an entirely different one altogether. Do not simply give up; be persistent in this, you will thank yourself later!

As with the daily gratitude practice, it is important that you actually write these down. Because a practice such as this is also changing your neurology and training your vibration in a new, higher way, you will begin to notice that over time this becomes your natural way of thinking and being. For example, say your car breaks down on the way to work. Prior to engaging in this habit, you may have responded with a "What else will go wrong today?" and proceeded to have a terrible day. Adopting this as a habit, you may now find yourself saying, "What if this were a blessing in disguise?" continuing on to have the best day of your life.

I am not exaggerating. I cannot say it enough: our thoughts determine our perspective, which determines our behavior, and therefore determines our experience–every time. These habits are specifically designed to help you stay intentional and positive in your thoughts and perspective, ensuring a positive outcome. Do you grasp the freedom in that? We may not be able to control every event that shows up in our lives, but now you know of at least two ways to create your experience within the event, and a good experience at that. The implications of these tools are profound. They mean that, quite literally, you never have to be afraid of anything again. What might you do with all of that freed up energy?

Meditation

You knew this one was coming. It's kind of a no-brainer.

I'd be a fool not to include this as a daily habit. There's a reason why all of the spiritual leaders, teachers, and guides out there always seem to point their audiences to this simple, yet for some complex, practice. In my experience and observation, I have noticed that those spiritual seekers or awakened individuals who know meditation is good for them and want to do it consistently, but don't, are largely blocked by two reasons: they think meditation has to take an hour or more a day to have any effect, and they believe they are doing it wrong. I know that's where I started. I thought it had to look like focusing on your breathing and pushing all of the thoughts out of your head, which is ridiculous in and of itself because the word "pushing" implies resistance, and where there is resistance there cannot be allowing. I also thought that each meditation had to bring about some profound epiphany that took a long time of breath focusing and thought pushing to reach, and if I didn't have one then I didn't do it right or long enough. It was exhausting to think about so I pretty much just didn't do it. Does this experience sound familiar to you?

Upon speaking with many of my clients when assigning this habit, I learned I was definitely not alone in these assumptions. Fortunately for us all, I learned along the way that meditation doesn't actually have to be any of that. Quieting the mind through focused breathing might be a powerful way, and heck, it might be the thing to aspire to, but by simply pausing for a few minutes each and every day and focusing our attention inward, amazing things can happen.

Google the word "meditation" and you will come across countless studies done to prove its benefits, some of which include reducing levels of stress, increasing creativity and productivity, improving sleep, and enjoying higher levels of happiness and satisfaction. Many work places are even encouraging their employees to meditate, as research has shown that calmer, happier employees make for a more successful and productive workplace.

There are many ways to meditate, and the best way to do it is the way that feels good to you because that means you will do it consistently. Guided meditations, binaural beats, visualization, and even daydreaming are perfectly acceptable ways to meditate. They all focus your attention inward, raise your vibration, center and align you, and quiet the endless amounts of external chatter and noise in the world so you can think more clearly. This makes it possible to approach your life from a clearer, more intentional place. And while epiphanies and profound realizations and clarity do indeed occur during meditative states, if you happen to have just a nice quiet few minutes with yourself where you are still and open, you have received great benefit. It all adds up and contributes to your alignment, which is why it is included as a daily habit.

If reading the subtitle of this habit made you groan and already begin plans on how to skip it, I urge you to try a different approach. Choose a set amount of time that you can commit to meditating each day—something doable, like five minutes. Oh okay, three minutes. That way, if you do more than three minutes, great, but you will ensure that you are doing at least that much per day, and you can always work up to around 15-20 minutes if you like. Abraham-Hicks even say, in their "Getting into the Vortex: Guided Meditations" book and CD, that life is for living, not sitting in a cave and meditating all day, so their guided meditations are no more than 15 minutes each (I HIGHLY recommend those, by the way). Meditate in whatever format feels best to you that day, just make sure you are still and sitting up with your eyes closed. There is such a thing as a "walking" or "moving" meditation but that's not what we're talking about here. Over time you will find that this is one of the best ways to receive guidance and divine nudges from your guides and angels, as well as to develop your spiritual gifts and strengths.

Perhaps the most profound benefit I've noticed through meditating consistently is the strengthening and expansion of my relationship with myself. I like and love myself more, I have a higher quality of words chosen in my inner dialogues, and I am automatically more kind, loving, and gentle with myself when I experience something disappointing. I noticed as I began this practice consistently that it provided me with an avenue of really "seeing" and acknowledging myself each day. I was surprised to discover how much I had been avoiding really looking at the person I was depending on to create the wonderful life I so desired. I like to describe my meditations as making eye contact with my soul and not looking away, and whatever I see is embraced and accepted. It is incredibly healing, and has opened up more avenues than I knew existed. You want to know Who You Really Are? Meditate every day and meet yourself.

The structure for this daily habit is simple:

- Choose a set amount of time that you can commit to meditating each and every day, even if it's just three minutes. You can always do more than that, but choosing a realistic amount of time helps ensure your consistency with it. If three minutes seems too much, begin with two minutes, or even one. Just start somewhere.

- Sit up somewhere comfortable and quiet, and close your eyes. Set a timer, if you like, so that you don't have to worry about checking the clock.

- Meditate in any form that feels good to you, such as following a guided meditation, visualizing, day-dreaming, or quietly focusing on your breath. You can change it up each day, too, if that serves you.

- Release any expectations of what it needs to feel like, or what should happen in each meditation. Simply show up for yourself.

Journaling

You probably also guessed this one was coming. Hey, I'm already asking you to write down your gratitudes and powerful questions as part of your daily practice, I might as well get you to spend a bit more time with that pen in your hand, right? In fact, I usually begin my morning practice with journaling, because for me it is the thing that helps me click in the most and the fastest. Journaling is an excellent way to organize your thoughts, process emotions, and set intentions.

Like meditation, there really is no wrong way to do it, just what feels the best to you that day. Sometimes I chronicle what happened the day before, analyze a challenge I am having, or simply name feelings. Sometimes I write three sentences and other times it's several pages. The length doesn't matter, nor does the content, really. It simply matters that you show up for yourself in this way each and every day as a way to connect with that inner being who wants to become louder in your life.

I also want to point out for all of you Law of Attraction buffs that writing in your journal is a safe container to process those negative thoughts and emotions you are trying your best to deny, for fear that it will activate that vibration and draw more of it to you. First of all, that's not really how it works. Secondly, if you are having negative thoughts that you are suppressing in an attempt to be positive, then you essentially have negative energy stuck in your body that will eventually have to express itself, sometimes as a physical symptom or illness. Instead of condemning this part of you that sometimes has low moments and negative thoughts, allow it a safe place to go because it is a part of you and should therefore be honored.

The trick is to not stay there, as in writing it in your journal and then calling up your friend Sally Ann to tell her about it, and then Suzie, and then Sarah...you get the picture. Journaling can be incredibly therapeutic, and is an essential tool for managing one's thoughts, emotions, and vibration. It's very important to purge and let go, not continue to ruminate. That is why it is a daily habit; it helps you get ahead of these things that have previously caused your life and well-being to spiral out of control at times.

The structure for this is what I have already said: *write at least one sentence a day, and write about whatever currently feels good to write about.* If you're worried about someone finding it and reading it, type it out on a locked document on your computer, or just simply hide it better. But in all truth, as you move forward in this alignment process and become more authentically you, I guarantee you won't care about that. I fully expect my girls to come across my drawers of endless journals and take a peek one day, and that's okay with me. Heck, I leave the sucker sitting out open sometimes, which my husband could easily read. I'm pretty sure he hasn't yet, and I tease him for being such a goody-goody.

One final note on this habit: if you find yourself having one of those days where you can't seem to find even one minute to sit down and write your thoughts out, try talking to yourself (or your angels and guides) out loud. I thank God for Bluetooth in cars these days, because the car, as well as the shower, is my favorite place to have conversations with myself, my Cosmic Team, and God, and no one driving next to me thinks I'm a crazy person (unless they see my head bobbing). I also take solace that Albert Einstein himself said that those who talk to themselves out loud are some of the most emotionally intelligent people out there because they are adept at organizing their thoughts and emotions.

Incantations/Power Statements

This habit is comparable to using positive affirmations, but I like to describe them as affirmations on steroids. The main difference is that instead of just saying a positive statement hoping it eventually catches on, you are utilizing your physiology to actually create a desired state of being out of thin air. I was familiar with affirmations when I first learned this habit from my coach (I'm fairly certain it originated from Tony Robbins), but I often felt as if affirmations were simply "Band-Aids" giving me very temporary relief. When I learned how to engage my voice and body with the words, I was blown away by how quickly and powerfully I actually *felt what I was saying.*

The implications of this are astounding, and point to an underlying theme behind all spiritual work: *we do not need anything external to ourselves in order to feel a certain way, or to be happy.* This technique is the quickest and most efficient way I am aware of to be happy. I have said this before but it is such an important thing to understand that I will say it again: it is not the job, the house, the car, the career, the money, the relationship, etc., that we want. We want the feeling we think having these things will give us. Can you even imagine the freedom it affords you to be able to feel any which way you want in any given moment, just because you simply decided to?

This is, the way I see it, the key to conscious manifestation. Feel and practice the vibration of the thing you want and you will draw it to you that much faster. Or, further simplified, feel good as often as you can and you will allow in all that you desire. Incantations are an even more incredible tool when you become so adept at it that it no longer becomes about trying to manifest a given thing, but just because it feels good and just because you can. As a nice sort of side effect, the thing you thought you needed in order to be happy comes anyway via the Law of Attraction! How fun!

Practiced as a daily habit, this technique becomes an extraordinary intentional and conscious dance through life. When you hear the phrase, "You are a conscious co-creator," this is what they are talking about. And this is what I am talking about when I say that I know the worst of my life is behind me. Because I have learned, practiced, and consistently experienced the power I hold, the power we all hold, to decide how we want to feel and how we want to experience any given thing, independent of the circumstance.

As I mentioned, our physiology plays an important role in this habit. You see, the mind does not know the difference between memory, imagination, and "reality;" it will produce the same physical response for all three. This is why memories of an event that occurred years ago can still bring you to tears, or you can get yourself all worked up over something that hasn't even happened yet. This is a profound thing to know about our human makeup because, when understood, we can use it to our advantage. Everyone teaching the power of visualization knows this. They understand that when one takes the time to make pictures in their minds about what they want, they are also practicing the feeling and therefore vibration of that desire, which causes it to come to them via the Law of Attraction. Our physical bodies are fantastic vessels because they will essentially do the work for us if we just sit and daydream a bit, or repeat a phrase with emotion and physical movement.

In fact, try smiling right now, for no reason at all. Go ahead, I'll wait (a little author's humor for ya). You may have noticed that you feel at the very least a tiny bit better than just a moment ago. Your brain responded to your facial muscles moving in the direction of a smile, and released the very same chemicals that get released when you are actually smiling about something specific. Neat, huh? With an incantation we use our physiology in combination with the words we are saying.

It feels good after you exercise, right? That is because the brain is releasing feel-good hormones and chemicals in response to your movement. Moving is a good thing. Energetically speaking, you can shift stagnant energy around simply by shifting positions or getting up and walking outside, or into another room. Our bodies like movement. So when you are saying a positive statement while moving, it is that much more powerful. Add in some intentional intonation and volume with your voice and you've got the means to manifest an emotional state nearly instantly.

This brings me to the structure of an incantation. In a nutshell, here is what it is and how to do it:

An incantation is a powerful state of being changer/creator that combines words of affirmation, your voice, and your physiology. This is an excellent and powerful tool to cause yourself to feel a desired way without needing specific circumstances to be in place. As a result, not only do you feel really good, you attract circumstances and experiences that match that feeling!

Step 1: Choose a statement or phrase that captures how you want to feel or be. This is your incantation.

Step 2: Say your incantation out loud, using emotion in your voice (intonation, rhythm, volume) much like an actor convincing you of their character.

Step 3: Stand in a position/stance that makes you feel powerful, or move in a powerful way (i.e., a yoga position, clap your hands, stand with feet apart and arms outstretched). This is called your "Power Move."

Step 4: Repeat your incantation with emotion out loud while in your power move until you feel what you are saying. This can take as little as a few repetitions to as many as twenty, depending on how you're feeling when you start and what kind of feeling you are wanting to create.

Although the explanation and mechanics of this are amazing, exciting, and profound, this is a habit with which not too many people are immediately comfortable. Over time, especially when done daily, it becomes much easier. I recommend starting with a simple statement of something you desire, but that you can already sort of grasp, such as *"With each day that passes money comes to me more and more easily"* versus making too big of a leap that only leaves you feeling frustrated, such as *"I am a multi-millionaire and am wildly successful."* There's nothing wrong with the latter statement; it's just probably one most have to work up to after some time getting comfortable with incantations. I chose examples of incantations regarding money to share with you intentionally, because, first of all, that is the number one topic clients bring up with me, and, secondly, using incantations to consciously shift my money vibration was one of the biggest catalysts to helping me earn a higher income. But you can use them around any topic or state of being you wish to call forth (see examples in appendix).

In addition to using incantations as a daily habit, I also use them prior to any coaching call, speaking event, or sometimes right before going somewhere like a party or even the grocery store *("I am focused, efficient, and easily find everything I need")* just to ensure that my experience is a good one, and get myself into a peak state of being. Why not, right?

Daily Inspiration

This last habit is very simple and easy to do, and I'm guessing many of you are already doing it. All it entails is reading, listening to, or watching some sort of inspirational resource that you resonate with. This can be anything that inspires and connects you; inviting you into the space of inner awareness … yep, you guessed it, daily. It doesn't have to be a lot; it could simply be reading from one page of your favorite book or listening to a YouTube clip from your favorite author or teacher.

I know you know how good you feel when you do this, and you now have a deeper understanding of what feeling good offers you, so if you're not doing this daily already simply begin to do so. Allow it to contribute to the merging of your beliefs, values, and highest intentions with your daily life, and give you a consistent reminder of Who You Really Are. It is quite effortless, yet is a very powerful way to get into alignment.

It need not take a lot of time and it doesn't even require you to sit still. I love listening to audiobooks while getting ready for the day or driving in my car, or listening to Abraham-Hicks' YouTube clips while cooking or cleaning. I also begin my day by opening my daily emails from NealeDonaldWalsch.com and reading the "On this day, I believe God wants you to know…" reminders, or Mike Dooley's daily "Notes from the Universe," which you can sign up for at tut.com. Both are short yet pack a huge punch. Sometimes I will read a few chapters of the current inspirational book I'm reading right before bed, or before I begin my other habits. It's different each day for me, and that's okay. Find what works for you and be consistent with it.

A final word ...

So there you have it, five of the most effective, impactful, feel-good habits for creating your foundation of living a life of alignment with Who You Really Are. They make it easier to feel good more often, and keep you steady when something unexpected shows up that could potentially knock you down. These daily habits are your path to consistency in your higher vibration. In other words, this is how you can access and be Who You Really Are.

I cannot stress enough that if this is the only thing you take away from this book, it will be enough to rock your world–if you take the daily part seriously, that is. I know I've been hammering the daily part to death; when I first started teaching these habits, many of my clients would come back to me after a few weeks of starting out reporting that it didn't seem to be working for them. I would then ask them if they were practicing each and every day, and of course, the answer was no. I am merely saving you this detour.

"Daily" truly is the magic ingredient of having a daily practice, which now seems like a no-brainer to me but five years ago was non-existent in my mind. There are, of course, other habits you can adopt, and you can find those in other books and resources like that of Tony Robbins or my very own coach's book, *Making Waves: How to Build a Successful Coaching Business During the Coaching Tsunami*, by Dustin Vice, where he details some of these same ones and a couple I didn't mention. And if you really need some accountability with this, I urge you to go beyond finding an accountability buddy and hire yourself a coach who understands this stuff and will lovingly kick your butt into gear. It is worth every penny and more.

As I said before, I typically challenge someone who isn't yet my client to try even just a couple of these out for 14 days straight just to see what it feels like. They almost always come back to me two weeks later with stories of how good they feel and how circumstances of their lives have even quickly changed, and want to hire me on the spot–it can happen that fast. I say "almost always" because the few who don't just simply assumed I was full of crap and didn't do them, or maybe they wanted to but weren't truly ready, which is okay, too. A seed has still been planted and their souls may have other things planned for this part of their journey.

Don't wait until you've finished reading this book. In fact, stop reading now, go out and buy yourself a nice, shiny new journal that makes your heart flutter when you look at it, and begin these practices today! Going forward, this new journal will be dedicated to completing the daily practices you learned in this chapter. Unless you'd like to postpone feeling awesome, exercising your abilities as a powerful, conscious co-creator, and watching things fall into your lap...

Practical Application:

To help you get started, below is a recap and a structure for creating your very own daily practice, and you'll notice that it includes a space for identifying what time of day you will commit to completing it. I highly recommend that time is first thing in the morning, as not only will it set the tone of alignment for the rest of your day, you will also feel a sense of accomplishment right away that will give you a boost of energy for everything else you have planned. It is also the time of day that is easiest to *create more time*. In other words, if you find yourself playing the card of "I'm too busy today" or "There aren't enough hours in the day," which can be really believable illusions, this is the time of day where you can make more space–as in get up 30 minutes earlier, or even 15 minutes is a good place to start.

I recommend you at least try it this way for a couple of weeks, and if at that point you recognize there is another time of day that better serves you, go for it. I've had clients who absolutely did not enjoy or prefer the morning for their practice, and it worked just as well for them to do it at another time of day.

Also, feel free to keep it simple, especially if this concept scares you a bit. I've suggested five spaces available to identify your habits/practices, but you do not need to use them all. You may want to start off practicing a few or all of the above daily habits that I've outlined, or you may want to choose some of your own. There is no wrong way to do this, as long as the practices you are engaging in are able to be completed daily and feel good in the doing of them. Feel free to copy the structure below in your own journal.

My Daily Practice Plan

Having a daily practice full of habits that feel good and support your alignment is perhaps the most powerful path to conscious manifestation and living a life of alignment with Who You Really Are. It provides a structure that harnesses your energy and flows it in the direction that you want to go in, keeping your focus and vibration high, free of distraction, and making it easier to recover when you fall out of alignment. The most important ingredient to a daily practice is that you complete all of your habits DAILY–commitment, consistency, and discipline are the magic words here. Because you are making this commitment to yourself and living a life of alignment, make sure you choose habits/practices that feel good and are enjoyable to you, AND are doable–you want to make it easy to create sustainability and longevity. Please create your "Daily Practice Plan" in your journal.

My Daily Habits–Numbered 1-5

The Time of Day I Will Complete Them (*It helps to put this into your calendar)

My Accountability Plan and/or Accountability Buddy's name

Space for "Other Notes"

CHAPTER 22
EMBRACE YOUR
VIBRATIONAL REALITY

"When I run after what I think I want, my days are a furnace of stress and anxiety; if I sit in my own place of patience, what I need flows to me, and without pain. From this I understand that what I want also wants me, is looking for me and attracting me. There is a great secret here for anyone who can grasp it."

~ Rumi

Once you have your daily practice established and are enjoying what it feels like to be centered, clear, and aligned, you will find it much easier to navigate the "path of least resistance." Because you are an energetic being whose reality is comprised of vibration, not just the physical things that you can see, hear, smell, taste, and touch, it is vital that you begin living your life from that awareness.

I recently attended an Abraham-Hicks seminar in Chicago, and laughed along with the rest of the audience when Esther Hicks (one of Abraham-Hicks's earthly spokespeople) said, "You know too much, you cannot go back." We laughed because each of us in that room had reached a point in our spiritual awareness where we knew this to be true. It is impossible to go back to your old way of thinking and being, and to your old life's paradigms and structures that you have released. Since they will no longer work for you, you may as well work towards embracing your newly discovered vibrational reality and find a way to consciously live within it.

Hopefully now you are a bit more accepting of your humanness and your negative thoughts, as well as beginning to see how it all contributes to the whole. We've talked about this idea of resistance a lot so far and I want to make sure I give you a clear idea of exactly how you might live, practically, in terms of vibration. As spiritual beings having a human experience, we are subject to the natural ebb and flow of life. In fact, we naturally ebb and flow throughout each day, just like we have an array of both positive and negative thoughts and emotions throughout each day. And, just like we talked about it not being the goal to eliminate negativity altogether, this isn't about eliminating those natural ebbs, either, or avoiding the very challenge and contrast of life that enables us to grow and evolve so well. It's about learning how to allow yourself to get into the flow more often, as well as learning to "flow within the ebb."

The latter is a different kind of flow, not necessarily marked by the joy, gratitude, happiness, relaxation, contentment, and enthusiasm one tends to feel when they are really "flowing." It's more like a form of surrender, that relief you feel when you just let go of fighting what is. There are several ways to do both, so let's take a look at a few of my favorites, shall we?

Follow What Feels Good

This phrase has become very popular in recent years, and does have a way of bringing almost immediate relief. I say it all of the time, especially when someone is appealing to me for quick advice for a decision they are making. Sometimes, I see them relax instantly, knowing what to do next; they just needed to hear someone else say it or be given "permission." Other times I can tell they want to throat punch me, as they likely think to themselves, "What a cop-out answer. Follow what feels good, what the hell does that even mean?!" (I read energy, remember.) I get their frustration, especially if I know they don't understand the mechanics of following what feels good, yet. Covering my throat for protection, I then attempt to explain a bit more deeply.

"Following what feels good" is most useful if you are doing so from a place of alignment, or feeling clear and centered. *If at any given moment you ask yourself what feels the best, without stopping to calibrate your vibrational or emotional state, you may get an answer, but it may not be an accurate one.* In other words, what feels good in that moment is subject to which state of being you are in.

If you are angry after a disagreement with a co-worker, for example, and you pause to ask yourself what would feel good in that moment, you may very well get the answer of "throat punch them"–sorry, I just really find that image to be funny and entertaining. Now, I think we can all agree that this is probably not the best answer, and will not yield you the highest results. However, if in the same scenario you decide instead to remove yourself from the situation, or table it until you are in a better-feeling place, and then ask yourself what would feel good, you are likely to come up with an answer that is more aligned and serves your highest good (and doesn't involve physical violence). Do you see the difference between the two?

It is in this context that this can be one of the most powerful "laws" to follow on your path of connecting to, and being, Who You Really Are. When teaching this concept to my clients or students, I also speak of it as a way to access and strengthen your internal guidance system, your soul's voice, or intuition. *Conversations with God* says that "feelings are the language of the soul," which really makes sense to me. In other words, when you are feeling any kind of emotion that falls under the category of "bad"–angry, sad, frustrated, stressed, overwhelmed, depressed, panicked, anxious, scared, or just plain "off"–you can look at it as your soul or Higher Self alerting you to the fact that your current thought or perspective is not representative of your highest truth. Conversely, when we feel good our soul is telling us we are in alignment with whatever is before us.

This is a very useful and practical piece of information, especially in everyday life. It can create a very powerful experience of mind-body-spirit connection, simply by paying attention to how you are feeling in any given moment and *trusting it*. But remember, in order to be able to trust what you are feeling, alignment is the name of the game. If you are simply drowning in emotions that resulted from being in a more reactive state of being, you will have to do a bit more digging, and have some patience.

This concept is also particularly useful when you find yourself in an ebb, or what some might describe as a "funk" or a bad mood. It's easy to identify and follow what feels good when you, well, feel good. It's a bit trickier to do so when you don't. It's important, therefore, to be aware of your context, or "vibrational environment," when you are using this approach. For example, if you are a woman and you are experiencing the difficult part of your monthly cycle, what "feels good" in that context might be to cry, take a nap, or eat a pint of ice cream. Following through on those urges not only honors what you are feeling, but it is also incredibly self-loving, and allows you to "flow within that ebb" more easily.

The Art of Avoidance

Avoidance is a skill that is misunderstood and underrated. When used properly, it can be highly effective in terms of attempting to consciously manage your thoughts, emotions, and vibration. We are generally taught the value of confronting and dealing with anything difficult that comes our way head on, but we rarely stop long enough to question if something is in our highest good at the moment. Of course, nothing is black and white and I believe everything is subject to context, so sometimes avoidance is what we might call a "bad" thing and of course sometimes addressing something head on can be useful and powerful, too. Knowing how to discern what's best in any given moment is key, and is why I like to refer to this as an art.

Do you ever notice that when you find yourself to be tired, moody, crabby, overly sensitive, overwhelmed, or anxious, your view of the world changes? You tend to see things in a vastly darker or more pessimistic perspective than when you're generally feeling good? And have you ever noticed that when you've indulged in thinking about or acting on those things from that lower state of being, it not only made things worse but prolonged the experience of feeling that way in the first place?

The most common example I find that people relate to is when you find yourself ruminating and obsessing over things late at night, usually when you are trying to sleep. A thought about something you forgot to do that day pops into your head, and no matter how small that thing actually is it seems to be the biggest deal in the world to you in that moment, and you can't manage to let it go. It then invites other thoughts like it: "*I forgot to pack little Charlie's school library book today, and I'm pretty sure it was due. Was it due? Oh God, I think it was due. His teacher is probably really annoyed by that, and poor Charlie, he was probably so embarrassed when everyone else was turning their library books in on time but him. I am such a bad mom sometimes, why can't I get simple things right? It doesn't help that I was preoccupied by that deadline at work. There is no way I am going to get that one done on time, either. Seriously, how am I going to get that done on time?*"

All of the sudden you are trying to "problem-solve" from a tired, low, and limited vibration, where you are perceiving your current thoughts about it from a very distorted perspective. Somehow you manage to fall back into a fitful sleep, and when you wake up in the morning and step out into the light of day, things all of the sudden don't seem so bad.

Ever have that experience? This is where avoidance would be highly useful.

I use this sucker All. The. Time. Like, pretty much every day. Because it is almost a given that at some point during the day we find ourselves in an ebb, a moment where we are feeling tired, have lower energy, or we come across something that, for better or worse, simply annoys the crap out of us. And if we engage in subjects of importance during those ebbs, which happens because apparently we are gluttons for punishment, it inevitably creates a bit of unnecessary drama and even sends us down an emotional path we didn't intend on going down. It simply does not serve us to give it any energy from that state of being.

The very best thing one can do in that moment is take a deep breath and make the decision to table whatever you are thinking about that is causing such stress. Avoid it at all costs, actually, as there is absolutely no benefit in torturing yourself for something that you are currently not in a resourceful enough state to effectively deal with. When you are vibrating that low, your perspective is off and you are in a state of "imagined truth," as Neale Donald Walsch refers to it, and you quite literally don't have access to the resources, answers, inspiration, and ideas to help you make a good choice or see things clearly. So why waste your time trying to force it? It's akin to attempting to swim upstream or run uphill; both activities are marked by resistance, and when you try to fix a problem from a lower state of being you are simply engaging in and inviting more resistance.

This doesn't mean you have to avoid problems indefinitely, although I would be remiss to deny that things often work themselves out when you do. You can always come back to the topic at hand when it serves you to. Put simply, come back to it when you are feeling good again and are more resourceful. Either wait until you get in that aligned state or, even better, work consciously to get there by looking for things to feel good about. In the meantime, use every trick in the book to avoid focusing on things that aren't really as dire or urgent as they seem in that moment. I prefer the art of napping, personally.

Trust me, if there is any skill to master in life it is this one. Even from a neurological perspective this makes sense; when the brain is flooded with stress hormones, it doesn't work as well (I've said this a lot, I know, but I really want you to get it). In a neurological scan, the best "thinking" parts of our brains don't light up as much as they do when the brain is flooded with "happy hormones." Your brain is not in optimal "problem-solving" mode under these conditions, so it makes sense to do something that gets it there first.

That's why taking deep breaths is such a powerful stress-management tool; it provides the brain with much-needed oxygen so that it can function better. Following this logic will save you countless unnecessary downward spirals of negative emotion and/or bad choices and experiences, and will position you for doing your very best in all situations. It will invite Who You Really Are to come forth more.

Get into Alignment and Then

This one works hand-in-hand with the art of avoidance. In fact, it is essentially the same thing but with less emphasis on avoidance. It is more of an overall approach to your life, a proactive one at that, and this alone will help you navigate the natural ebb and flow with much greater ease, leading you to optimal results in any situation. What I mean by "get into alignment and then" is, as you may have already guessed by my heavy use of this language, feel good first and then go about your task, your challenge, or your day, or any segment of it. When you understand that you are at your best physically, neurologically, mentally, emotionally, spiritually, and energetically when you feel good (that is, calm, centered, clear), you can trust your decisions, no matter what they look like. Not to mention you are accessing the flow of well-being that is available to us all in any given moment, which is really the point, isn't it?

What that might look like in an average "real-life" sort of day is beginning your day with a practice that centers and connects you, as I've discussed in several chapters, so that you can move about your day already aligned with your highest intentions. It can look like hitting the pause button when you notice yourself feeling off or upset by something, and stepping away to recalibrate and assess what would feel good to focus on instead. It can look like taking breaks frequently, like going outside for a few minutes several times throughout your day, taking a nap, meditating for a minute, or laughing with a friend, and then coming back to the task at hand. It can look like following what feels good and trusting it.

One of my clients has a wonderful habit of setting her alarm on her phone a few times throughout the day to remind herself to check in on her state of being, and mentally lists gratitudes and appreciations to raise her vibration. Sometimes she even goes into the bathroom at work to meditate for a minute or two, which I think is brilliant. Getting into alignment first looks like handling a difficult situation, discussion, or decision from a better-feeling place because you know that when you do so you are inviting in the best possible outcome.

A participant in a workshop I gave was so struck by this idea that she actually had the words "Align and then ..." tattooed on her forearm! Talk about a permanent reminder! I went a less gutsy route and had a ring made by a very talented friend of mine, with the words "Get into Alignment and Then ..." written inside a large, glass bubble for myself, and each of the coaches that I've trained in my Spiritual Alignment approach.

If you make it your focus and only job in life to feel good as often as possible, to engage in as many things as you can in your life from a place of alignment first, you will have mastered this being human thing. These are, of course, a work in progress for us all, but the more you practice the better you get.

Choose Easy

I can get on board with the notion that "easy" is not always the best choice, especially in terms of "taking the easy way out" versus rising to the challenge. Oftentimes, the "hard way" is full of things more vital to our growth than the easy route, and upon looking back we are very happy we chose it, right? Yet I am also a **big** fan of "easy" and "ease" in general; they are among my highest values and you can bet your behind that if there is an easy way I will find it and choose it. I openly admit that I always seem to find myself on the hard path by "accident," never by choice.

I'll let you in on a little secret–I have known that life is supposed to be easy my entire life. I say "secret" because I quickly learned growing up that nobody else around me thought that way; every person in authority made sure to tell me that life is difficult, and I certainly didn't want to argue with them. Don't get me wrong, I have absolutely experienced life as "hard" more times than I'd like to recount, and I'm certainly not saying that it doesn't often feel that way for most, if not all, of us. I am saying that despite my experiences of it being hard, I still knew it didn't have to be.

I had this, I don't know, "feeling" we'll say, that there is a way to experience the ease and flow of life and there is never a moment where we don't have access to it. It is never withheld from or denied to us, and we don't even have to earn it. As I grew in my consciousness and self-awareness, I made it my goal to have ease be my dominant experience of life. I decided, "Sure, we can throw in the hard stuff every now and again to keep myself sharp, of course, but let's go ahead and make ease the largest part of it."

I have a feeling I could write an entire book about this topic alone, but for the purpose of embracing your vibrational reality, I'll just say that it's okay to choose easy sometimes. It's okay to choose easy lots of times, actually. If there's an easy choice and it honestly feels good to take it, ya know, you can just do it. What do you have to prove by taking the more difficult route, and to whom do you have to prove something?

I know this sounds simplistic and perhaps even a bit silly, but man oh man, do we make some things in life harder than they have to be sometimes. Usually we do this based on misperceptions of how things should be or what we feel is expected of us.

Perhaps I can convey what I mean by this concept of "easy" better through a specific example. When I became a mother, I automatically assumed many of the traditional roles and expectations that I thought came with it without even thinking. This was a curious thing because my husband and I certainly didn't participate in the notion of typical gender roles in our marriage. In fact, he has always had to deal with a lot of "I don't do that" from me when it came to certain household chores like vacuuming, bless his heart. But with marriage, I knew how I felt and what I believed. With parenthood, I had no idea what I thought so I simply adopted what was already laid out for me by society and history: I should put my coaching career on hold and be the one who is home with my daughter. I should not only be okay with that, but also be happy to spend my days solely focused on her. I should easily be able to juggle all things motherhood without so much as a complaint because it's my job and, well, if I don't like it I shouldn't have had a kid in the first place. Yeah …

It didn't take long for my soul to very loudly inform me that I wasn't in alignment with this set of beliefs, and the Universe set into motion all the right circumstances, experiences, and contexts that helped me clearly define what I did believe and want out of parenthood (i.e., contrast-filled experiences). So, we put my daughter in daycare, and not only did I give myself the time and focus to build my coaching career into what I wanted it to be, I used that time to take care of things that were just simply easier to do without her with me. While other moms dragged their screaming kids with them to Target and on other errands, I did my shopping while she was at daycare. While other working moms had a day off from work and therefore kept their child home with them, I sent mine for at least part of the day anyway and took care of the endless amount of things that needed my attention, including self-care. When invited to parties and gatherings that didn't fit with the routine of our daughter and our family, my husband and I simply declined.

Why? Because it was easier. And in this case it was the path of least resistance, therefore it was easier for us to be happy, even if some people didn't understand these choices. Is it the right choice for everyone? Probably not, but that's why it's up to each of us to decide what that looks like.

So that's what I mean by be willing to "choose easy" as you navigate your vibrational world. Don't make things harder than they need to be, especially if you're just trying to appease the judgment of others. Relieve yourself of any obligations, structures, or paradigms that feel hard, and let it be easy instead.

Flowing within the Ebb

Just a final word on this idea of learning to flow within the natural ebbs of life. As I stated earlier, this is a natural part of the human experience. You are going to encounter the experience of ebbs throughout your life no matter how evolved and aware you become, just like you will with negative thoughts and emotions. They are all a part of it, what we came here for, and there is something comforting about knowing and accepting this as you move forward with your life. I find that it's not so damn jarring when you have an unpleasant experience. The relief you feel when you realize you aren't royally screwing up or losing at this game is a tremendous gift.

So embrace those ebbs; they are there to serve you. They always hold a divine higher purpose, and it isn't necessary for you to identify it right away. Relax into what is right in front of you as often as possible, and the fear and anxiety that used to drive a large part of your human experience will be replaced with trust, ease, and a heckuva lot more flow.

Practical Application:

As with everything I offer you in this book, don't simply take my word for any of this. Put on your researcher's hat, experiment with it yourself, and come to your own conclusions. I recommend taking one of the above techniques per day and "trying it on" for the whole day. Practice it, pay attention to what you notice, and write it down in your journal.

For example, spend an entire day following what feels good to you. Use some sort of visual reminder, even if it's just a simple rubber band on your wrist, to remind you to pause to ask yourself, "What would feel good now?" several times throughout the day. Each time you remember to ask yourself this, switch the rubber band to your other wrist. At the end of the day or the next morning, write in your journal what you noticed from the day.

I know it seems like a lot, but the more you do it, the more natural, effortless, and habitual these ways of being become, and the closer you will merge with your Highest Self.

CHAPTER 23
CHOOSE AUTHENTICITY

"Close your eyes and imagine the best version of you possible. That's who you really are, let go of any part of you that doesn't believe it."

~ C. Assaad

Even though the overall theme and message of this book screams authenticity, I felt it was still important to dive into this aspect of being Who You Really Are more deeply and practically. The path of authenticity is what we all strive for, no matter our background, belief system, values, or goals in life. Every discomfort we feel in social, personal, or professional situations is our soul begging for it, and each time we feel really good about ourselves, our soul is celebrating it. There is no greater experience than being authentically you, and in order to experience more of that, you need to know what it looks, feels, tastes, smells, and sounds like.

I feel like inauthenticity comes from wanting to fit in and be safe; it's about survival. Adapt to your surroundings or you won't belong; fit in at all costs or suffer. It isn't usually until the pain of *not being* authentic begins to outweigh the pain of *not fitting in*, that people are motivated to change. I suspect it's also just as much about the fear of "being seen"–allowing others to see Who You Really Are.

But I believe everyone has a yearning to be authentic, to be their true selves, without effort or apology, and I also believe that everyone has the ability to. I recently listened to Brené Brown's audiobook, *The Power of Vulnerability,* and she really cleared something up for me. She said that there is no such thing as purely authentic and inauthentic people; there's no "you either are or you aren't." She said that authenticity is a choice, and that we all at different points in our lives have chosen to be one or the other–no one is exempt from either experience.

Furthermore, she articulates that in addition to being a choice, being authentic is also a practice; in other words, it's a choice you make several times throughout each day. There will be moments throughout most of your day where you may catch yourself resorting to old patterns and ideas of who you are, as we've identified that there are ebbs and flows throughout one's day. Falling back into those old patterns isn't the important part, what you choose to do with it once you've become aware of it is.

What Authenticity Means

I'll give you my take on it. Authenticity means being yourself without effort, without thinking, and without filters. It means naturally being congruent with your values, truths, and unique qualities, and it means allowing your true self to be seen without apology. Authenticity does not necessarily mean positivity, though, or feeling all sunshine and lollipops all of the time, because to be authentic is to be yourself, and you, my friend, are human.

Being human means feeling emotions from both ends of the positive and negative extremes and everything in between, and being authentic means being willing to feel and be present with all of them. If you're upset about something but you don't admit it or voice it, then that isn't very authentic, is it? Being authentic in such a situation means voicing your true thoughts and feelings without defense or attacking another, but rather naming and putting your feelings out there, for better or worse, simply because that is what is currently present inside of you. Sometimes it means walking away from something that you aren't okay with and not saying anything at all. It also means being willing to disappoint others who want you to be someone different than you are, and being willing to be uncomfortable for the sake of your authenticity.

Authenticity is being who you want to be, versus who others want you to be, at the risk of not being liked or accepted. Therefore, along with authenticity comes a bit of fearlessness, mindfulness, and of course, vulnerability. I would also describe it as getting out of your human head and leading from the soul. Yeah? Good. Moving on.

Practicing Authenticity

In addition to adopting a set of daily practices and habits that whisk you into and help you stay in a state of alignment more easily, there are countless other ways to practice being authentic. But first and foremost it takes willingness, self-awareness, and conscious intention. In other words, ya gotta want it and ya gotta be willing to pay attention, like, all the time. Getting good at being authentic is not likely to happen independently; you're the only one who can make it happen **for you**. If you're on board with that then let's begin by identifying a few key elements and set up sort of a "structure" within which to practice your authenticity.

Identify your people. I find that, first and foremost, re-evaluating the people with whom you choose to spend the most time helps a lot. If you're hanging out with people around whom you feel it's a struggle to be yourself, or who make you feel inferior in any way, it's definitely going to make it more difficult to access your authentic self. Sometimes it's not necessarily the other people at all, it's more the assumptions you are making about them that can hinder you. But as with everything, I recommend starting with the path of least resistance. You can tackle the hard stuff later.

In high school, I was that person who didn't necessarily fit into a stereotypical crowd or group, but rather I dabbled in almost all of them. I found that not knowing who you are makes it difficult to choose a main crowd or commit to specific identifiable characteristics. But just as I was beginning to realize that fitting in wasn't all it was cracked up to be, I began to notice which group I enjoyed being with the most. Soon enough, those were my peeps. In fact, they are my closest friends to this day and our kids even play together.

My point is that once I noticed with whom I felt naturally at ease, I had a context to more safely "practice" being authentically me. I was able to notice how I was similar and how I was different, and began really embracing and being okay with my unique traits that I didn't simply adopt from someone else. Had I chosen to spend the majority of my time with a group I felt I *should* be a part of, I'm not sure that would have happened as easily.

Ask yourself, *who* are your people? *Why* are they your people? And *how* can you show up more fully as your authentic self when you are with them?

Identify your triggers. Knowing what causes you to go into inauthentic mode is pretty handy info when you're working on being more authentic. Is it certain people?

Particular situations? What makes you want to crawl under a rock and hide? Where do you find yourself "faking it" the most? What areas of your life do you beat yourself up about, or feel guilt around? Where does it feel effortful instead of effortless?

For me, meeting new people in social situations has always been a trigger for inauthenticity. My chameleon powers come out before I even know it, and as I am noticing their energy I am almost as quickly emulating it, if I'm not too careful. Other triggers that are common for many include feeling uninformed or unintelligent when engaging in conversations with others, running into people from your past and automatically reverting back to the person you were when you knew them, being in unfamiliar situations or territory, and comparing yourself to others. I still experience that last one in the context of motherhood. That's a big one for any mom, I imagine. It's why I avoid mom groups like the plague. But even when discussing parenting with my close friends and family I sometimes still find myself saying things like "I always make sure I am giving my kids as healthy of food options as possible," when in all reality my 6-year old may have eaten a Pop-Tart for dinner the night before.

Identifying your triggers doesn't necessarily mean avoiding the hell out of them, although that certainly helps and I actually highly recommend that you do to some extent. It is more about bringing in self-awareness and conscious intention, so that you can begin to be proactive, versus reactive, in these situations. This eventually makes it easier to show up as the highest version of you that there is.

Create your authenticity strategy. Once you are aware of some of your triggers and tendencies, it is super helpful to decide ahead of time how you are going to show up authentically the next time you encounter them. This could look like coming up with a mantra, or a power phrase that reminds you of your authenticity, that you can repeat prior to or when you are in situations that trigger inauthenticity.

This is something Brené Brown recommends as a result of her research on vulnerability. Her mantra for authenticity, "Choose discomfort over resentment," is one I love and have adopted for myself, because I would much rather be uncomfortable for a little bit than spend gobs of time and energy resenting others and myself for my choice to be inauthentic. I love this strategy because I use mantras all the freakin' time for practically every freakin' thing, and encourage my clients to do the same. I see mantras as cultivating more empowering, positive self-talk, and if you've got an inner dialogue going that supports your alignment then you are setting yourself up for this authenticity thing to be a real breeze.

Another strategy is writing out a script that you can use for common situations you find yourself being inauthentic in, and practicing them. Seriously. This was useful early on in my coaching career, as I was figuring out the parts they don't necessarily tell you about in training, such as when a client is chronically late for the call or a payment, or decides it's okay to eat their lunch during the session, chewing loudly the whole time. Having not yet fully come into my own as a coach, I frequently erred on the side of politeness with such things, acting as if their "food sounds" didn't bother me or that it was totally okay to be two weeks late with a payment for the third month in a row because, you know, they just didn't get to it.

With one particular chronically late-paying client, I found myself feeling awful every time I said, "It's okay, no worries, just get the payment to me when you can," especially because I was dependent on that money. The client consistently being late, and nonchalant about it at that, made me feel like he wasn't fully committed and didn't value our work together. By not authentically expressing how I felt and what I needed from this client, I was choosing to avoid the both of us feeling uncomfortable, or me being judged as money-hungry or greedy. As a result, I was betraying myself. It felt awful, and I yet did it again and again.

This topic came up when I was having a session with my own coach, and upon getting very clear that I wasn't showing up authentically in this matter, we devised a script for the conversation I was going to have with my client because, well, I was terrified to have it. We kept it smooth and simple: "Client, I'm noticing a pattern in your monthly payments being late, and I need to remind you that my policy is that you pay on time or the coaching sessions will be suspended until you do. I really enjoy our work together, and would like to continue it, but I also need to know that you are fully committed to this process with me." The client apologized profusely, even begged me to continue our work together and promised to be on time from now on, which he was. It doesn't always work out that way, mind you, but my takeaway was feeling really good about honoring myself and being authentic.

Other elements of a good authenticity strategy could include using a visual reminder, like a piece of jewelry, a sticky note on your bathroom mirror or car dashboard, or putting the word "authenticity" or your chosen mantra as your screen saver. I've had clients use a metaphorical "pause button" for when they encounter their inauthenticity triggers to help them remember to take a breath and allow their authenticity to take the lead. Feel free to come up with your own and play with it, there's no wrong way to do it.

Practice non-judgment. You should never judge any-body, ever, and if you do then you are not spiritual and are surely not an authentic person.... If I could use emojis in this book I would insert the winking smiley face one here, or give it a LOL. Don't worry, I am not going to sit up here on my spiritual coach pedestal and convince you to give up judgment altogether. That would be a) neglecting the human part of this whole message about being Who You Really Are, and b) pretending like I don't judge people all the time, too.

Instead I'm going to offer you a subtle adjustment in your approach to judgment: go ahead and keep on judging peo-ple until the cows come home, and don't try to force yourself to stop cold turkey. If you did that, you'd just feel even worse about yourself the next time you catch yourself doing it, and you'd be resisting the whole "I am gloriously human" con-cept. No, I'd like you to keep doing what you're doing *and* begin practicing a bit of non-judgment. That is, intention-ally look for situations where you can turn your knee-jerk judgmental reactions into *observations* as they arise, and then turn them into something good that raises your vibration to a level where you can once again access your authenticity.

The difference between an observation and a judgment is that an observation is a noticing and an awareness of something with no negative or positive emotion attached to it; it is a neutral energy. A judgment is loaded with emotion, positive or negative, and impacts the "judger's" experience depending on the emotions attached to it. When we choose to stay in judgment we are essentially choosing to live in that energy and experience it ourselves, because we are feeling the emotions assigned to it. But when we move into observa-tion, we are neutralizing that energy and giving ourselves a choice as to where we'd like to go next.

I'll give you an example. My client, Jessica, was dealing with a difficult co-worker at her new job, who appeared to be treating her rudely and dismissively for no reason. On one particular day, this co-worker wouldn't even get up from his desk, which was only a few feet away, to come speak with her when he needed to, sending her short and abrupt emails instead. Jessica said she could feel the familiar feeling in her abdomen, that thick, dense, and dark energy rising steadily up to her solar plexus, then chest, then throat. She could feel herself going into judgment mode, making up all sorts of things about how he was a misogynistic jerk and must hate women, a train of thought she could've easily continued on with. However, she caught herself quickly, noticing that her current thinking did not feel good, which was an indication that something was out of alignment. We had been working on the "pause button" strategy for such things, and Jessica chose to use it in that moment.

Right there at her desk, Jessica began to shift out of judgment and into observation mode, knowing that she wanted to feel better. She asked herself, "What have I observed has happened here?" Her answer was that she observed a human being doing his work in a way that she perceived as unfriendly. This observation was neither right nor wrong, it was just what happened. She didn't include her own personal meanings and attachments to the observation, nor did she draw any conclusions about it. Neutralizing what happened through the power of observation took the sting out of the situation for Jessica, which allowed her to feel better about it and consciously choose where she wanted to go next, versus continuing to react.

She chose to make up that this co-worker's behavior had nothing to do with her, that he was perhaps going through a rough time and she didn't need to take any of it person-ally. In fact, she could choose to feel compassion for him. Donning this new perspective, Jessica was able to go about her work and barely noticed her co-worker's behavior. She chose to be nothing but warm and kind whenever they did interact, and returned her focus to her own work and well-being afterwards. It wasn't until weeks later that she learned he had been going through a bitter divorce and preferred to keep to himself.

What does practicing non-judgment have to do with being authentic? To use the example above, had Jessica con-tinued to follow the path of judging her co-worker to be a rude jerk, she would have ultimately caused herself more unpleasant experiences by spending more time feeling bad, and perhaps acting in ways that were not true to Who She Really Is. She would have likely acted in a way that she learned from society that says, "If someone wrongs you, you wrong them right back," rather than coming from the truth of her being, which says, "You are love, they are love, and we all come from and deserve love."

When you stay in judgment too long, you simply can-not access authenticity. Getting into the practice of non-judgment and using it as often as you can allows you to access your authentic self frequently and easily. Plus, you know, you shouldn't be so judgmental (smiley emoji).

Practice mindfulness. Finally, you can practice choos-ing authenticity by practicing mindfulness. The Oxford Dictionary defines mindfulness as "a mental state achieved by focusing one's awareness on the present moment, while calmly acknowledging and accepting one's feelings, thoughts, and bodily sensations, used as a therapeutic tech-nique." It is so much easier to access your authentic nature while you are present and aware of the factors and aspects at play. When you slow down, breathe, and notice your surroundings–you, quite literally, see more.

Brené Brown takes it a step further in her book, *The Power of Vulnerability*, where she describes it as allowing yourself license to feel your feelings fully, without labeling yourself. I really love this take on it, because not only does it indicate self-awareness, it implies having a choice in who you want to be and where to go next at any given moment. Just because you've paused long enough to notice and connect with what you're thinking, feeling, what your physiology is doing, and what's happening around you, it doesn't mean you are owned by any of it.

Practicing mindfulness can look like a lot of things, but I'll give you some common examples of what it looks like for some of the people I work with to help you decide what it looks like for you. Mindfulness looks like stopping what you are doing in any given moment and taking inventory of life happening in and around you. It can look like putting down your phone, or not running around your house taking care of different tasks, and sitting down for a moment in the quiet. It can look like asking yourself questions about how you're feeling or what you're thinking, taking deep breaths, meditating for a moment, journaling, focusing on gratitude, or simply looking around your immediate surroundings for things to appreciate.

I do the latter in the car, especially. We drive so much and it's so easy to get annoyed by the traffic, the driving of others, or be in the state of mind of "I've got to get to where I'm going, got to hurry, and I'll be happy when I get there." So to counteract that tendency, and also just because it's a nice time to be with myself and reflect, I'll turn off the radio and begin noting out loud all of the things I pass by on my drive that I think are beautiful, interesting, and enjoyable.

It gets me so present and is an instant vibration-raiser, not to mention that it quiets the inevitable mind chatter that tends to take over when I'm not paying attention.

Mindfulness is a great practice full of countless gifts, not just the gift of accessing your authenticity more easily. It magically slows down time, and lifts layers of life's illusions instantly. It tells you secrets that no one else knows, and reminds you that everything you need is right here, right now. It is the core essence of the daily practices outlined in the beginning of this section, because being mindful and aware is the most direct path I know to close the gap between who you are as a spiritual, energetic, vibrational being and who you are as a human being in this world of the relative. It's the most effortless one I know of, too, which is why there isn't a client who hires me who doesn't do this, and why I have made it my foundation for living my own life.

Start telling the truth about Who You Are, and everything else for that matter. I saved this one for last because I knew it would get the most groans and perhaps be the scariest part. Am I right? Yet you can't skip over it and manage to be authentic, you just can't. Authenticity is synonymous with truth telling. When you're not being authentic, you are not telling the truth, and vice versa.

My advice for this one is to just start telling the truth as often as possible, to as many people as possible. When you catch yourself making something up in order to not hurt someone's feelings, such as "No, I'm sorry, I can't make it tonight, something came up at work," when you really are just looking forward to a cozy night at home, choose to put your feelings first, instead. You are not doing them any favors by lying to them, and chances are they can tell you're lying and will then begin making up all sorts of non-true assumptions about why that is, causing them to feel bad.

Do not betray yourself in order to not betray another–that is essentially what is happening when you do this. *Conversations with God (Book 1)* says, "betrayal of the self is betrayal nonetheless. It is the highest betrayal." Lying about something, or holding back out of fear of what others will think, is self-betrayal. In short, not telling the truth is being inauthentic, and being inauthentic feels bad. When we feel bad, we are not in alignment with Who We Really Are, and are not our highest, most resourceful selves. It is a lose-lose situation for all involved. So make a commitment to tell the truth as much as possible, catch yourself and be gentle when you're not, and simply make a new choice. Do this consistently and it will become second nature, and authenticity will become your dominant vibration.

Practical Application:

Take some time to identify and work with some of the above suggestions, as well as adding in any others you may come across or come up with on your own. Do not skip this part. You cannot be your authentic self without bringing awareness to who you are and what that looks like, and remember, it is a choice that takes practice implementing.

Please answer the following questions in your journal:

1. Who am I when I am being inauthentic? What does inauthenticity look like for me?
2. Who am I when I am being authentic? What does authenticity look like for me?
3. Who are my people, the ones I find it easiest to be myself around? Who are not my people?
4. What are my biggest triggers to inauthenticity? Where do I show up as inauthentic the most?

5. My "authenticity strategy" is …
6. Some frequent thoughts of judgment that I'd like to turn into observation are …
7. I will practice being mindful by. …
8. My other thoughts and insights about authenticity are. …

Chapter 24
Start Telling a New Story

"Are there things in your life that are as you want them to be? Keep telling that story. Are there things in your life that are not as you want them to be? Don't tell that story. Look and speak in the direction of where you want to be, not where you are or where you were."

~ Abraham-Hicks

This is one of the most important pieces of the puzzle of living here on Earth and one of the most vital parts of the equation of being a spiritual being having a human experience. When you break it down, we are all creators of our own reality because we are all storytellers. Thoughts and words are creative, so what we say, the story we tell over and over again, becomes what we see in our daily lives.

The "story" that I am referring to is comprised of the words you think inside your head, or your inner dialogue. It is also the words that spill out of your mouth when speaking to others about any given thing. Your actions, observations, and expectations tell your story, too. Remember the energetic signature concept from a few chapters ago? Your signatures tell your vibrational story. The Universe receives your story through your vibration, and the Universe begins reflecting your story back to you immediately.

One cannot keep telling the same story, focusing on the same things that don't feel good, over and over again, and expect to have a new experience. It really is that simple, yet it appears to be not so simple when it comes to working the story to our advantage. This is because we all keep talking about the things we don't like, that we are outraged about, and that we are against and annoyed by, instead of talking about the things that we love, appreciate, and are for. And because we insist on talking about what we don't like, it only results in us having more of these things to talk about. We feel justified in our feelings, so we continue talking about them, telling everyone we can, and are reluctant to get off the topic.

I'm not exactly sure why we do this, why this has become a cultural habit, and I have been just as guilty of it, too. But I also know that when I take the time to pay attention to my thoughts and work to shift them by paying attention to something that feels better, my story quickly changes. It isn't a "one and done" sort of thing, as in you change your thoughts once and your story is forever changed. It takes nearly constant focus; living on autopilot absolutely must become a thing of the past. Yet it doesn't take much intentional focusing for you to begin to immediately experience the rewards.

The Nuts and Bolts of Changing Your Story

To make this a doable endeavor, I am going to outline some focus points for changing your story. It's important to recognize that this is not an all-or-nothing thing; any dent you can make in shifting some of those 60,000+ thoughts a day you have in a positive direction will have a noticeable impact, so allow yourself to feel good about any effort you make.

1. *Be willing.* Willingness is everything. If you are not willing to recognize and admit that you are indeed telling a story that is not in alignment with Who You Really Are and the life you say you want, then you have zero chance of changing it. But if you are willing to recognize your creative role in all of this, and are willing to begin seeing and doing things differently, then you have energetically given yourself access to countless resources from which you had been cutting yourself off when you were stuck in resistance and denial.

2. *Choose a new perspective.* One of the most powerful questions you can ask yourself when attempting to experience something in a new way is "What is a better way of seeing this?" Whether this is posed as a powerful question, one of the daily habits outlined a few chapters ago where you let the Universe do the answering, or you answer yourself right away, you have now begun practicing a new, higher vibration around the topic at hand. All of our thoughts, emotions, behaviors, and actions come from whichever perspective we are currently holding, so the more you can consciously choose a perspective that feels good to you, the more your thoughts, emotions, behaviors, and actions will effortlessly follow suit.

3. *Use positive self-talk as much as possible.* Your inner dialogue, or the way you speak to yourself *about* yourself and the world around you, has a tremendous impact on your energy and well-being. It can be a sneaky thing, too; many people don't even realize how much they are bashing themselves or how negative their views are inside their own heads, especially if they are striving to appear to be a positive person on the

outside. You cannot hide from your thoughts, and you cannot hide your thoughts from the Universe. Yet instead of attempting to monitor all 60,000+ thoughts a day you are having and avoiding a trip to the loony bin, try being more proactive with them. This is where the energetic signature tool really comes in handy; it allows you to write a script that you begin to memorize, which becomes the vibration you are practicing and replaces your old negative inner dialogues. It brings consciousness, awareness, and intention into the picture, and that triple force can move mountains. Practicing the daily habits I've outlined for you will also transform your inner dialogue, especially practicing gratitude, powerful questions, and incantations.

4. *Be mindful of what you are saying to others about yourself and your life.* A great rule of thumb to use is: if what you're saying doesn't feel good coming out of your mouth, it is not a story you want to tell. It's one thing if you are processing some news you've received or something upsetting that just happened, and you're talking it out with a trusted friend or writing about it in your journal. As discussed before, that is completely fine and a very useful way of managing your energy. But the part you have to be careful about is what you choose to do from there. For example, if you get into a car accident and you feel shaken, of course you are going to need to talk about it with someone in order to move forward. But if you mention it over and over again, talking about it every time you are about to get into a vehicle or anytime someone else brings up a topic even remotely related, then you are telling a story that is not congruent with what

you really want, in this case, being safe. I once took an in-person workshop with Wayne Dyer, who suggested paying attention to which words follow your "I am" statements. Each time you hear yourself saying "I am_____," ask yourself if the words that were in the blank space align with the story you want to tell or not. He went on to explain that the words "I am" are the two most powerful words we can use to consciously create, so be intentional with the words you choose to follow them. This, of course, applies to your self-talk and inner dialogue, too.

5. *Actively look for the best qualities and aspects in yourself, others, and the world around you.* The biggest culprits contributing to telling a story about your life that doesn't line up with the one you want are the negative things you focus your attention on most of the time. As I've already said, we humans tend to focus on the stuff that is wrong, lacking, or bad in life. Watch your local news station and you'll see what I mean. But when you make it your business to look for the good in life, you will see more good in life. Why would you want to waste your time on anything else? One way to actively do this is to acknowledge your higher self constantly, noting your best qualities, accomplishments, and efforts. Write them down, as suggested in the practical application I gave in Chapter 11: Be your own BFF, or fall asleep listing them in your head. You can do the same thing with other people and situations. Bring it into your consciousness and awareness by writing them down or speaking these aspects out loud. In fact, tell the other people you appreciate them, you will probably make their day!

6. *Disengage from drama.* Simply avoid it. Scroll past the posts on Facebook that are depressing or are trying to suck you in, excuse yourself from conversations steeped in drama, and certainly, don't initiate drama yourself. If it is a drama that involves you whether you like it or not, do everything in your power to step back and allow the Universe to handle it. Also, be aware of the dramas you are creating in your own head, the stories you make up about things that have happened, or what someone said or did. If you're going to make something up about it, choose something that feels good. Finally, choose kindness over being right. Speak lovingly, truthfully, and peacefully whenever possible.

7. *Tell a new story based on what feels good.* This component also requires flexibility and a willingness to adapt in the moment. It is mighty tempting to keep your focus on what is, rather than what is possible, and sometimes it is so satisfying to talk about present, unwanted conditions because we feel justified in our disdain for them, and we want the validation from others. But that satisfaction is short-lived, and leads us down a road that we tell ourselves is not of our choosing. So in the moment, as much as possible, tell your story out loud and inside your head, through your words, behaviors, and actions, based on what genuinely feels better. Does it feel good to talk about how everyone in your life treats you like crap? Does it feel good to talk or think about how bad things always happen to you, or that you can never seem to catch a break? Does it really feel good to list all of the reasons or evidence as to why that is true? I'm guessing no, so what would feel better to

say about that? Perhaps something like, "I've been treated poorly in my past, but I am surrounding myself with more loving people now, and things are getting better." Over time, adjustments such as this will begin to create a new outer world for you, but as Abraham-Hicks teaches, *Tell the new story with the purpose of feeling better now, not to sway the outcome, and the outcome will take care of itself.* Remember that your only job is to feel good, **now**, because that is how you come into alignment with Who You Really Are. And Who You Really Are is: divinity, love, and magic. The external stuff will follow, surely, but Who You Really Are knows that isn't the point.

Place your attention on these aspects as often as possible, keep telling yourself what an amazing being you are, and accept words of kindness and affirmation from others rather than deflecting the compliments. Keep your focus on what is possible and what you want, rather than what seems to be your current "reality." Know that it can change in an instant.

Practical Application:

Deciding ahead of time to be mindful of the story you are telling is the difference between agreeing with me and actually doing it. To be fair, we've got so much going on most of the time and many of us live such a fast-paced life that it's challenging to remember to implement these things in the moment. Thus, as discussed in previous chapters, knowing your "triggers" for falling into your "old story" pattern is crucial, as is being aware of what supports the new story about Who You Really Are that you want to tell.

In your journal, identify the following (I am giving you examples to help get your brain going):

1. **My "old story" that I am now willing and ready to change is:**

   Example: That I am at the whim of things happening to me and around me and that I have no choice in the matter. That I am not deserving of the life that I want, and will therefore be stuck in this experience of lack, low self-worth, and negativity forever.

   A more specific example: I never have enough money. I am always living paycheck-to-paycheck. Rich people are greedy, why should they get rewarded with all of that abundance when us good poor folk struggle to get by? There's no way out, either, as my current job has no room for moving up and it's too hard to try to start something new.

2. **The "new story" I am now willing and ready to begin telling:**

   Example: I am a powerful conscious co-creator, a divine being of love and light, an extension of God here to create, express, and experience myself in whichever way I desire. I am aware of and am highly capable of using the tools God gave me in which to do this. I love myself, I love this life, and know that it is always working for me.

   A more specific example: Like everything else in life, money is a form of energy, and I have access to as much of it as I desire. We all deserve abundance and wealth, and I am capable of shifting my attention, thoughts, and behaviors in such a way that connects me to the flow of it. I am unlimited, therefore there are no limits to what I can do, be, or have. If I want a new job or a higher income, I can let the Universe go about taking care of the details while I keep myself open to it by feeling good and noticing the abundance that is already all around me.

3. **My "triggers" for telling and living my old story are:**
   Example: Being around people who I feel inferior to, being tired or not feeling well, when something challenging arises, having to go to my job that I hate. ...

4. **Things that support the story I am now going to begin telling:**
   Example: Being around people of like mind, engaging in my daily practice, reading or listening to inspiring material that reminds me of Who I Really Am, taking good care of myself so that I feel good enough to access these truths more often. ...

5. **My strategy for telling my new story is:**
   Example: Disengaging from the drama and negativity around me, consciously creating a new energetic signature around the parts of my old story that I wish to change, listing things about myself that I love and appreciate each day, actively looking for and writing down the positive aspects of others and life around me. ...

CHAPTER 25
GIVE TO OTHERS

"Share of your abundance. Even if you think you are not
abundant, share what little you think you have. What else is
the point of having something if you don't want to share it?"
~ Neale Donald Walsch

Conversations with God says if you want to know yourself as
something, or experience a certain aspect of life, give
it away. In the giving of it away to others you are declaring
to the Universe that it is yours to give. I would be remiss
not to include this powerful truth in guiding you on how
to be Who You Really Are, because this very simple act fills
us with such love, happiness, joy, and satisfaction that it is
pretty much a straight shot to being your Highest Self. This
is also a part of your creative power, as Who You Really Are
is a powerful creator.

I can't tell you how many times I have been struggling,
hit with some wave of thought or emotion that threw me for
a loop or was just having a low-energy day, and upon giving
a coaching session or being a listening ear for someone else,
noticed I felt completely better. By giving away what I didn't
think I had access to, I was giving myself access to it, recon-
necting with and being reminded of my Higher Self.

In fact, anytime you find yourself in a funk, and you can't seem to find your way out, look to see how you can give to another. It doesn't need to be anything huge or dramatic. It can be a kind smile in a stranger's direction, or holding the door open for someone whose hands are full. It could be reaching out to a friend who you know has been going through a rough time and asking them how they are.

If you want to be and experience abundance, cause another to experience it. Donate to charity, even if it's just a few dollars, or share your food with someone.

If you want to be and experience clarity, cause another to experience it. Listen to someone as he or she processes and works things out, and offer suggestions if asked. Tell him or her what you see clearly in them.

If you want to be and experience goodness, cause another to experience it. Find ways to bring goodness into their day, like surprising them with a phone call or flowers.

Furthermore, it's no secret that our world is experiencing great upheaval right now, and there are many out there who feel helpless as to what to do about it. By giving away the things we feel are lacking in this world right now, such as love, kindness, understanding, compassion, tolerance, and empathy, we are not only directly contributing to the whole, we are expressing and experiencing Who We Really Are. And this kind of example tends to catch on like wildfire.

Who You Really Are is love, joy, peace, kindness, generosity, magic, abundance, limitlessness, understanding, beauty, and grace. Who You Really Are is any positive aspect of humanness you can think of. If you want to know yourself as any of it, simply give it away to another, and you will find yourself being it. The ripple effect of this is endless, too; by accessing and being any of these aspects of Who You Really Are, you are inviting others to do the same. The formula is fail proof. And by the way, this is how you "be the change you wish to see in the world," as the great teacher Gandhi encouraged us to do.

We are all one, so when we give to another, we are really giving to ourselves. When we give to ourselves, we are also giving to others. It is a beautiful, masterful plan... kudos to God for that one.

Practical Application:

Experiment with this one. What is it that you'd like to do, be, or have? What aspect of Who You Really Are do you want to call forth and experience? Choose one aspect or state of being each day for a week, and on each day, cause another to experience what you've chosen. Be creative, and remember that there is no way that is too small in which to do this.

Chapter 26
Rinse and Repeat!

"An ounce of practice is worth more than tons of preaching."

~ Gandhi

Guys, this all comes down to practice. We've all heard the saying, "practice makes perfect," right? I believe that with all things in life this is very, very true. All athletes know this. Even if you happen to have pure raw talent, practice is necessary to make you even better; even the best athletes in the world are required to go to practice every day.

As you continue to practice, it all gets easier. You get stronger. As you continue to place your consciousness and awareness on these things, they become more effortless. In no time at all, you will find that your life has taken on a whole new form, texture, feel, and even a whole new look.

As I write this, I am on day 1,749 of engaging in my daily habits and of making it my top priority to live my life from a place of alignment as much as possible. And life looks and feels so different from what I used to know that I can't even really remember what it was like before this. I remember it conceptually, but to even go back to my old way of thinking and feeling for a moment is too painful, too uncomfortable. I have such a low tolerance for feeling bad now that

I am motivated to do whatever I have to do to feel good again, because I now remember and know it as my natural state. Alignment and feeling good are now my dominant vibration. Any interruptions to that, no matter how small or seemingly minute, are just plain unacceptable to me.

Yet even after all of this time, I don't always get there right away. I think that's the beauty of it. Being steeped in the contrast of life, immersed in the discomfort, and then consciously working your way back to alignment brings such a feeling of relief that is so satisfying. I don't think it's about total elimination of the contrast, or the negative experiences. I think it's about working towards decreasing the recovery time. Over time, it takes less and less time to "bounce back," or get back into our natural state of alignment and well-being. And knowing that you are doing it quickly and simply with all of the resources you've always had inside of yourself, without needing anything or anyone external to you, is an incredible feeling. It is true power, true freedom, and true limitlessness.

There is a lot to remember on these pages and a lot to absorb and think about, so let me attempt to bring it down to the bare bones. You may want to copy the following and plaster it all over the place, where you will be reminded often:

How To Practice Getting in Alignment with Who I Really Am:

- My only job is to feel good now. The rest takes care of itself.
- Ways to feel good include: practicing gratitude and appreciation, asking powerful questions, meditating, playing, napping, looking for positive aspects, giving positive meaning to things, doing things I enjoy and

that bring me pleasure, giving to others, positive self-talk, reading, watching, or listening to inspiring, feel-good material, being present with loved ones... the list goes on. Remember that what feels good depends on the context, so always ask myself, "What would feel good to me now, in this moment, exactly as I am?"

- Be conscious of when I don't feel good (i.e., impatient, annoyed, heavy, upset, sluggish, lethargic, etc.) and be voracious about making adjustments to feel a little bit better, until I find myself easily swept back into a state of alignment.

- Embrace what is, rather than resisting it. Embracing allows me to relax, which puts me in a more resourceful state to take action from a place of alignment.

- The How is not up to us; it is the Universe's job to take care of the details. Our job is to know what we want, and feel good as often as possible to stay in a state of allowing.

- Always get into alignment and then deal with the task at hand. If something is upsetting to me, or I know I am in a lower state of being upon dealing with something, I need to get off the topic until I can return to it from a state of alignment.

- Tell the story of Who I Really Am, not who I used to be, through my thoughts, words, behaviors, and actions. Discern what those look like based on what feels good to me.

- Be authentic, speak my truth, yet soothe my words with peace, about everything and to everyone.

- Follow what feels good, follow the path of least resistance, and I will effortlessly be led to where I want to go.

I know there are a lot of teachers in the spiritual and self-development fields that like to offer fail-proof formulas to help you get to where you're going, and it can be frustrating to try one on only to see that it didn't "work" for you. The reason for this is that because of the complexity of our beings and the countless factors and influencers that make up who each of us is, it is impossible to find a "one size fits all" approach. However, I'm going to offer you a formula that condenses all of this even further, and makes the application of being Who You Really Are that much more simple when you find yourself swimming in the deep waters of human circumstance, events, and interaction that can often make it hard to see straight. While this formula is also not a "one size fits all" approach, it has become a Godsend for me, and subsequently, those I've coached who are deeply immersed in this work. Make adjustments to it according to what makes the most sense to you.

The Alignment Formula:
1. *Get into a state of alignment.*
2. *Follow what feels good.*
3. *Back off from what you are focusing on when you notice yourself not feeling good, and shift your attention to getting back into alignment.*
4. *Repeat as necessary.*

Keep practicing, keep choosing alignment, and when it all seems overwhelming and like it's too much to remember, just bring it back to feeling good. Feeling good is your gateway to alignment, and alignment is your access point to being Who You Really Are. It is from this place that everything takes care of itself, and all of the sudden you know what to do and/or how to proceed.

CONCLUSION

I was driving home from giving a workshop with a dear friend and colleague this past January. It was the final commitment I had to complete before turning everything off to give my full attention to completing this book, and it was a fantastic one on which to end. The workshop had been small and intimate, yet was filled with people who were ready and eager to begin living life from a much more authentic and conscious place. The transformation that had taken place in the roughly seven hours we had spent together diving into material very similar to what you've just read was awe-inspiring and humbling to witness. I was flooded with feelings of relief, appreciation, gratitude, joy, love, and inspiration. As my co-facilitator, Jennifer, had said, I felt "well-used."

As I tend to do in the car, I was talking out loud to my Cosmic Team, decompressing and processing all that had transpired and all that was gained. There was a transformation in me, too. Through giving what I knew to others, I became full of myself. No, really, I felt so full of Who I Really Am in that moment that tears stung my eyes and I began articulating out loud how much I love and enjoy being me. I realized that if I were a character in a movie and I was someone watching it, I would want to be my character the most. Know what I mean?

And you know that voice that butts in whenever you happen to allow yourself to feel good about yourself? The one that says, "Whoa there lady, I think you're getting too big for your britches!" It didn't even show up, and honestly I think that's the first time that it hasn't. I was so completely comfortable with loving myself in that moment; it was like seeing your best friend in the whole wide world for the first time in years and feeling so excited and happy about it. To give you perspective, I had only just started having these kinds of moments within the last year or so, and I was still just getting used to it. This was by far the loudest and most powerful moment.

As I was having this love fest with myself, my Cosmic Team decided to chime in by placing a shooting star just above my line of vision at that very moment. I was driving and, of course, watching the road, not even looking up at the sky. But there it was, fast and bright and catching my attention and eye instantly. I hadn't seen one in years, yet here was one, seemingly placed there especially for me.

I burst into tears at that moment, accepting gratefully the validation I had just received. Being that my very name describes a shooting star, and one of the first readings I had ever received from my guides began with them addressing me as "an amazing, blazing star," there couldn't have been a more perfect symbol to get my attention. To me, my Team was not only agreeing with what I had been saying out loud, they were giving me the okay and encouragement to continue feeling that way. It didn't have to be a fleeting moment I later rationalized or talked myself out of.

I love that kind of living. I love the serendipity and synchronicity, I love watching everything unfold perfectly and seeing that perfection even when things don't always look like anything I wanted or originally intended. I can think of no better way to live than dancing with the magic of the Universe and soaking in the joy of being Who You Really Are, even if it's just in glimpses here and there at first. Once you notice and acknowledge them, it's no-holds-barred from there on and the cosmic dance quickly becomes the new norm.

As I said before, I am by no means done with this work, or "there" yet; I don't believe there is an end point, just more expansion. But I do believe that once you have certain pieces of the equation down, such as bringing consciousness, awareness, and intention into each and every day through surrounding yourself with things that support and emphasize Who You Really Are, everything comes together so much more easily. And you simply can't get it wrong. As a bonus, all of that human stuff you once found to be so trying and difficult becomes more satisfying and even playful. Just keep going with commitment, consistency, and discipline. Feel good as often as possible, for no reason at all, other than caring deeply about how you feel, and knowing it's the most direct path to your true essence.

You are a spiritual being having a human experience, and you are also a human being having a spiritual experience. Both views afford you the opportunity to have an extraordinary life on this planet, and if you prefer to travel the path of ease, flow, alignment, and enjoyment, then I urge you to get really good at:

- Embracing what is, even if you don't quite understand it yet;
- Loving yourself as best as you can exactly as you are in any given moment;
- Feeling good as often as possible so you can access all that you need to be Who You Really Are;
- Following and trusting what feels good to you; and

- Allowing the Universe to take care of those pesky details called "the how."

If any of this sounds overwhelming or just out of reach for you, I assure you that the only thing you need is a willingness to start. The energy of willingness is such a powerful energy, and is at the core of every great change and transformation that occurs, every incredible desire that comes to fruition. And the best part is you don't have to do any of it perfectly! You can be human in all your glory and "screw up" as many times as you want! The best thing I ever read was that "we can't lose at this game." What a relief!

So go ahead and put this book down now. You've taken a very important first step by reading and engaging in it, plus you have a lot to process. Don't worry about the integration of everything in these pages, or anything you've learned of value anywhere else; a lot of it will happen unconsciously and even effortlessly. Yet don't put off the practical application part, either; don't leave yourself swimming in the land of concept for too long.

Show up for yourself every single day. If you want to meet your higher self and begin merging your energy together, if you want to feel the joy of being Who You Really Are in very functional, everyday ways, you have got to show up. The Universe will let you know what to do next, if you allow it.

Thank you for joining me on this ride, for giving me a small part of your focus and attention on your journey. I am eternally grateful, and if I've helped even a little bit then I am happy. Now, if you'll excuse me, I am about to go watch The Walking Dead and eat Chinese food in my yoga pants with my husband, but before I do, I will leave you with these parting words of encouragement and validation:

"Know that Consciousness fluctuates. It does not remain constant simply because it has reached a certain level, but increases and decreases depending upon the amount of the Soul's Awareness that is integrated into the Mind's Experience at any given Moment. Or as one observer put it: 'Enlightenment is not like getting your tonsils out—once it's done, it's done. Enlightenment is a moment-to-moment experience. That is both the challenge and its delight. The Quest is never over, and it is never boring.'"

—Neale Donald Walsch

BIBLIOGRAPHY

Brown, Brené. *The Power of Vulnerability: Teachings of Authenticity, Connection, and Courage.* Sounds True, 2013.

Brown, Brené. *Rising Strong.* New York: Spiegal and Grau, 2015.

Hicks, Esther & Jerry. *Getting into the Vortex Guided Meditations CD and User Guide.* New York City: Hay House, 2010.

Lakhiani, Vishan. *Code of the Extraordinary Mind.* New York, Rodale Inc., 2016.

Vice, Dustin. *Making Waves: How to Build a Successful Coaching Business During the Coaching Tsunami.* Palo Alto: 650 Productions, 2014

Walsch, Neale Donald. *Conversations with God: Book 1.* Charlottesville: Hampton Roads Publishing Company, 1995.

Walsch, Neale Donald. *Happier Than God.* Charlottesville: Hampton Roads Publishing, 2008.

Walsch, Neale Donald. *Home with God in a Life That Never Ends.* New York: Atria Books, 2006.

RESOURCES

Support:

www.novawightman.com Sign up to receive additional tools, resources and guidance on your alignment journey. This is also where you will find the opportunity to receive a 30-minute complimentary coaching session with a coach mentored and trained by Nova Wightman in her Spiritual Alignment Approach.

www.cwgconnect.com For free access to a variety of content from Neale Donald Walsch and other contributors.

www.nealedonaldwalsch.com For free Daily Inspirational Emails from Neale Donald Walsch.

www.abraham-hicks.com For free Daily Inspirational Emails from Abraham-Hicks.

www.tut.com For free "Notes from the Universe" from Mike Dooley.

Examples of Powerful Questions:

- What is the most amount of pleasure I can stand today?
- What would it look like to be completely in love with myself?
- How can I be loving and kind with others and myself today?

- What will my life be like after 40 days of practicing these habits?
- What would it feel like to be completely present and focused?
- Who is the highest version of INSERT YOUR NAME?
- What am I truly capable of?
- What would be possible for my life if I were able to master my emotions?
- What gift do I have to give the world today?
- What would it be like if I were to unleash my power with full abandon?
- What does it feel like to make $_____a year?
- Who would I be today if I weren't feeling crabby/sad/ irritated?
- What opportunities are available to me today?
- What if I were to focus purely on pleasure today?
- How can I connect even deeper?
- What is one step I can take towards my vision?
- How can I feel more passionately about my life?
- What relationships make me feel alive, engaged, and understood?
- How can I create more joy in my relationships?
- What's my life's passion that I want to manifest?
- What activities can I do that make me feel happy?
- What steps can I take to feel closer to the people I love?
- What kind of impact would I have if I reached my full potential?
- What would it be like to hear divine guidance clearly all the time?

- What if I were able to focus easily and be productive joyfully and with enthusiasm?
- How can I make myself a perfect vessel?
- How is what I'm doing now positively impacting my future?
- What if there was no such thing as obligation?
- Who am I as a powerful leader?
- What gifts will I be able to share with others after these 40 days?
- What magic lies within me that I don't even know about yet?
- What would it feel like to be unconditionally loving and unconditionally loved all the time?
- What is the next level for me?
- What if I had exactly what it takes to be who I want to be and do what I want to do?
- How can I be in a state of allowing today?
- How can I see the divinity in myself, and others, more?
- How can I reflect each person's love and beauty back to him or her?
- What miracles are awaiting me?
- What does perfect trust look and feel like?
- How can I move through fear and doubt quickly and gracefully?
- What if it were easy and fun to let go of my limiting beliefs and replace them with new ones?
- What is the gift in this situation?
- Of what am I really capable?
- Who am I really?
- How can I balance and nurture both my male and female energy?
- What is standing in the way of joy/love/abundance/success right now?

- What if there was nothing to worry about, ever?
- What if I had the capacity, ability, and know-how to be, do, and have anything I want?
- What would this day look like if I were to infuse it with joy, fun, and ease?
- What would be possible if I didn't believe in limitation?
- What does my clear picture look like?

Examples of Incantations:

"It is easy and fun for me to be authentic with myself and others."

"I am confident, and inner knowing comes easily to me."

"I happy and content with my life, and I love who I am."

"I am a spiritual being having a human experience. My soul knows what she's doing, and I trust in the perfect order of things."

"I am tuned in, tapped in, turned on and in perfect alignment. All is well."

"I am the personification of abundance." (You can replace abundance with anything you like–joy, love, peace, etc.)

"I am a money magnet. I attract big money and lucrative opportunities effortlessly, getting paid handsomely to do what I love to do and am so very good at."

"It is all working out better than I have ever imagined."

"I will let whatever happens be okay, I trust in the perfect order of things."

"Thank you, God, for helping me to understand that this problem has already been solved for me."

"I easily accept love, peace, kindness, abundance, and joy into my life."

"I am willing and ready to allow my brilliance to spill out of me. I am joyfully in love with myself and my life. More please!"

"I am the one I have been waiting for."

"I have a burning desire—an inner flame that will not be extinguished by outer forces—to know and live from higher regions, to be transformed so that my new concept of myself will no longer include any limitations. I am willing to challenge and change any thoughts that impede me from having a higher vision of myself."

"I have the power to change my life, and I am doing so now. I love all of the good habits I am learning, and I watch my life respond to my positive thoughts. If I had known how easy this would be, I would've started this process years ago. I am in awe of the power of my own thoughts to heal my body and my life."

"I, INSERT NAME, call forth the most divine inner love and wisdom within me, and invite it to shoot out to the rest of the world. I am willing to be a beacon of light, and feel and be that love."

"I, INSERT NAME, will reach into the depths of my soul to bring loving kindness to all that I meet. I am willing to see myself and others as who we really are."

"I, INSERT NAME, am a more powerful being than I can even imagine. I am ready to allow that power to shine through me even more now. I easily attract the people, things, and opportunities I want, and I easily redirect my attention on the positive when it strays. I can do, be, have, and create anything I desire."

"I, INSERT NAME, accept and love myself as I am. I am beautiful, magnetic, and am capable of bringing great joy and healing to the world. And there is nothing outside of myself that I need to do this."

"All that I want and need flows into me in oceans of abundance. Every day I continue to grow stronger. All that I need is within me. I am healthy, wealthy, confident, full of love, and dedicated to achieving my goals. Today I am whole and I can do anything. I am grateful for all the bounty, beauty, and well-being in the universe and appreciate all who give and receive these gifts. With each breath I am inspired, my consciousness awakens, and I feel energized."

"I, INSERT NAME, share and expand love. I now command my subconscious mind to attract the right people. Change lives! Be smart. Be fast. Bravely move forward. Lead. Defy the odds. Believe. All I need is within me now. All the love. All the passion. All the joy. All of the happiness. All the certainty. Here I go!"

"I, INSERT NAME, am a God guided expression of happiness, health, wealth, and joy for myself and virtually everyone I have the privilege of touching their lives. All that I want, desire, and need is instantly manifested and is flowing into me in oceans and oceans of abundance as I continue to create even more abundance for all to enjoy. I'm grateful beyond measure and appreciative of all that has already flowed to my team and me. I'm healthy, happy, wealthy, excited, congruent, confident, and full of pride as I'm committed to the pursuit of happiness for myself and all that I love. I believe life is exactly what you make of it so I dare to make it magnificent."

ABOUT THE AUTHOR

Nova Wightman

Nova Wightman is a Certified Life Coach (CPCC), NLP Practitioner, Reiki Master, and a Conversations with God Coach on Neale Donald Walsch's team (author of the Conversations with God Series of Books). Also the owner and operator of her own coaching company, Go Within Life Coaching, Nova helps spiritual seekers become spiritual rock stars by blending their spirituality with their humanity so that they can enjoy the crap out of life. She puts her clients on the fast track to conscious manifestation by teaching them how to align with Who They Really Are consistently, all while feeling joyful and satisfied along the way! A mother of two beautiful little girls, wife to her soulmate, and a 5th degree Master Instructor in Tae Kwon Do, Nova enjoys lots of quality family time, Netflix binging, and playing hide-and-seek. For more information or to contact Nova please visit www.novawightman.com.

Made in the USA
Coppell, TX
23 January 2022

72137900R00164